Boswell, Burns and the French Revolution

THOMAS CRAWFORD

THE SALTIRE SOCIETY
1990

The publisher gratefully acknowledges
the financial support of the Scottish Arts
Council in the publication of this volume.

Designed and produced by
Fianach Lawry Associates/Ruari McLean
Printed by
W. M. Bett Ltd., Tillicoultry

Contents

In memory of

Frank Brady
(1924-1986)

a great Boswellian
who meant to write
on this topic.

1. *The Meeting that Never Was*

Boswellians often speculate about the near misses — encounters with genius or notoriety — which Boswell might have had or could have had; they have even been known to invent imaginary conversations, such as the hoax interview with Kant which once took in a German professor who treated it as a serious source. One meeting which did not come off or, if it did, was not worth recording, was with Casanova, who was in Berlin at the same time as Boswell in 1764. Another, seemingly, was with Robert Fergusson; in view of what we know of their convivial habits it seems incredible that they did not meet in Edinburgh between 1772 and 1774, Fergusson's most creative period. But the Cape Club, of which Fergusson was the "laureate", is not mentioned in the Journals; and neither is Walter Ruddiman, Fergusson's publisher, though Boswell had once toyed with the idea of writing the life of his uncle, Thomas Ruddiman, Latinist and antiquarian. All this seems most extraordinary when we consider that Fergusson sent Boswell an inscribed presentation copy of the 1773 edition of his poems.[1] If he put it aside unread, it means that he completely ignored the presence, in the very city in which he practised as an advocate, of a genius superior in intrinsic literary power to almost all the poets of contemporary London except perhaps Goldsmith and his adored Johnson. And it means, too, that he was completely unaware of what the Scottish vernacular was capable of in the poetry of the city. True, he had himself written Scots songs, and very good ones; and true, also, that he had praised *The Gentle Shepherd:*

> I spoke of Allan Ramsay's "Gentle Shepherd", in the Scottish Dialect, as the best pastoral that had ever been written; not only abounding with beautiful rural imagery, and just and pleasing sentiments, but being a real picture of manners; and I offered to teach Dr Johnson to understand it. "No, Sir, (said he,) I won't learn it. You shall retain your superiority by my not knowing it."[2]

But the vernacular revival since Ramsay's time seems to have passed him by. He knew of Burns's existence, but was not curious enough to read him unsolicited, let alone go out of his way to meet him.

The nearest their paths came to crossing can be documented from a letter of Burns to Bruce Campbell, Laird of Mayfield and Milrig in Galston Parish, Ayrshire, dated 13 November 1788. Campbell was Boswell's cousin and "agent", and his wife may have been a relative of John Wilson, the printer of the Kilmarnock edition. Here is what Burns wrote:

> I inclose you, for Mr Boswell, the Ballad you mentioned; and as I hate sending waste paper or mutilating a sheet, I have filled it up with one or two of my fugitive Pieces that occurred. – Should they procure me the honor of being introduced to Mr Boswell, I shall think they have great merit. – There are few pleasures my late will-o'-wisp character has given me, equal to that of having seen many of the extraordinary men, the Heroes of Wit & Literature in my Country; & as I had the honor of drawing my first breath almost in the same Parish with Mr Boswell, my Pride plumes itself on the connection. – To crouch in the train of meer, stupid Wealth & Greatness, except where the commercial interests of worldly Prudence find their account in it, I hold to be Prostitution in any one that is not born a Slave; but to have been acquainted with such a man as Mr Boswell, I would hand down to my Posterity as one of the honors of their Ancestor.

The "ballad" can only have been "The Fête Champêtre", about an open-air supper and ball held on the banks of the Ayr in July 1788, at which Boswell's daughter Euphemia was present, to celebrate the coming of age of William Cuninghame of Enterkine, Tarbolton, though its real aim was political. As the poet's brother Gilbert later explained: "A dissolution of parliament was soon expected, and this festivity was thought to be an introduction to a canvas. . . . [But] Mr Cuninghame did not canvas the county."[3] Burns's first stanza begins appropriately enough by mentioning the three candidates – Sir Adam Fergusson, Colonel Hugh Montgomerie, and Boswell, and its reference to Boswell as Johnson's companion on the tour to the Hebrides is pithy, to say the least:

> *O wha will to Saint Stephen's house,*
> *To do our errands there, man;*
> *O wha will to Saint Stephen's house,*
> *O' th' merry lads of Ayr, man?*

> *Or will we send a Man-o'-law,*
> *Or will we send a Sodger?*
> *Or him wha led o'er Scotland a'*
> *The meikle URSA MAJOR?*

The letter is endorsed by Boswell: "13 Nov 1788 Mr Robert Burns the Poet expressing very high sentiments of me." Whatever the "one or two fugitive pieces" were, we have no record of their effect on Boswell. An earlier incident in the campaign, however, provides a further slender link between the two, with its own peculiar irony. In August 1788 Boswell was in Ayrshire, "canvassing the county". One evening he called at the home of Robert Baillie of Mayville, the father of that Lesley about whom Burns wrote one of his most beautiful songs:

> *O saw ye bonie Lesley*
> *As she gaed o'er the Border?*
> *She's gane, like Alexander,*
> *To spread her conquests farther.* (Stanza 1)

Burns did not meet her until 1792, when he thought her "the most beautiful, elegant woman in the world" (To Alexander Cunningham, 10 September), declaring himself to be "in love, souse! over head & ears, deep as the most unfathomable abyss of the boundless ocean" (To Mrs Dunlop, 22 August). History does not report what Miss Baillie thought of the poet, but she did put on record her impressions of Boswell in a letter to her friend Jean Campbell Reid: "I instantly fell a sacrifice to the charms of his wit, vivacity, and humour . . . I am *charmed, fascinated, bewitched* beyond the power of language (at least any language *I am mistress* of) to express, and wish, most devoutly wish, that I had a dozen votes at my disposal for his sake."[4]

Burns and Boswell, then, had the slightest of contacts. Burns wrote, hoping for a meeting; he does not seem to have got even an acknowledgment. The occasion of their near miss was a parliamentary one; but it had nothing to do with ideology, for it arose merely out of Burns's poetical comment on the social glee which gilded election-eering in those days. Politics was off-stage, but it was the politics of local interests and alignments, not of clashing principles and warring systems.

2. *Boswell to* 1789

Boswell was almost twenty years older than Burns and came from a very different family and social background. Far from being "a very poor man's son", as Burns described himself, Boswell was a scion of the landowning class and the legal establishment. Pride in his ancestors was always a prevailing sentiment, even during his apostate years in England. By 1749, when his father succeeded to the estate, there had been eight Boswell lairds of Auchinleck since 1504, and there was a blood connection with the Auchinleck family itself, which had held the barony for at least a century before that. His mother, Euphemia Erskine, was a great-granddaughter of John Erskine, Earl of Mar and his second countess, a second cousin of James VI, who had Bruce blood in her veins. To quote from Frederick Pottle's succinct summary:

> Boswell was descended from the Earls of Arran, Caithness, Kincardine, Lennox, and Mar, and from the progenitors of the Earls of Carnwath, the Dukes of Hamilton, the Earls of Loudoun, and the Earls of Wigtown. Among peers contemporary with himself, he was third cousin twice removed to the Earl of Buchan, fourth cousin to the ninth Lord Cathcart, third cousin to the third Earl Cowper, grand-nephew to the eighth Earl of Dundonald, second cousin once removed to the ninth Earl of Elgin and Kincardine.[5]

On his continental tour he called himself Baron Boswell, and developed as one of his many rôle models the idealised image of a Spanish grandee ("Be Spaniard; girl every day", Boswell's Memoranda, 20 February 1765). No doubt Boswell identified with David, the fifth laird (d. 1661), a Royalist who "waited on" Montrose after the Battle of Kilsyth and refused to sign the second Covenant although Ayrshire was almost totally committed to the Covenanters. But the sixth laird, also a David, was of the opposite persuasion to the fifth: in 1678 he was summonsed for "withdrawing from the ordinances in your own parosh and for being present at house and feild conventicles". In the late seventeenth century the neighbourhood seems to have been solidly anti-establishment: in 1688 the tenants of Auchinleck were required to sign an obligation not to attend field conventicles, and in 1691 a minister called to the parish declined because the heritors (and not, be it noted, the kirk-session) had accused him of "prelacy".[6] The Whig-Presbyterian strand in family tradition came to a head in the views and personality of Boswell's father, Lord Auchinleck; it was therefore inevitable that the biographer, in view of his extreme Oedipus complex, should incline to the Tory and Jacobite side.

But Boswell was nothing if not ambivalent, see-sawing between conflicting positions, and holding contradictory views and feelings in suspension at the same time. He came to intellectual awareness as one of the 1755-60 generation of students. These were years of anglicisation: of the Select Society, one of whose aims was to improve the "manners" of Scottish society; of Adam Smith's course on rhetoric (which Boswell attended); of moderatism in the church and opposition to predestination; of Hume's *History* with its striving for a "pure" style purged of Scotticisms; and, in the early 1760s, of Thomas Sheridan's lectures in Edinburgh for young men who wanted to acquire a correct and genteel pronunciation (Boswell went to these too). The whole thrust of these influences ran counter to the earthiness, the plebeian democracy, which (however Jacobite and Tory its earlier practitioners may have been) seem inseparable from the vernacular revival. There was still another influence on Boswell's generation, but one which is difficult to document – an enthusiasm for French writings similar perhaps to a later generation's fascination with Marx and Lenin. Boswell and John Johnston of Grange, and perhaps his other life long friend from these years, W. J. Temple, celebrated their culture heroes on Arthur's Seat by chanting their names into the wind: "Voltaire! Rousseau! Immortal Names!" – at the precise time when the luminaries of the first *Edinburgh Review* (1755-56) were considering broadening its scope to treat of works by d'Alembert and Rousseau in the third volume, which never appeared.[7] As happens continually down the centuries, university students were among the first to experience new political emotions, even if they were as young as fifteen or sixteen, and even if they had not actually read anything by the sages they worshipped.

Boswell's continental tour of 1763-6 enabled him to indulge both Tory Jacobitism and also, paradoxically, libertarian sentiments. His Jacobite enthusiasm goes right back to childhood: he was five when Prince Charles entered Edinburgh and slept in Holyrood. The boy "wore a white cockade, and prayed for King James, till one of his uncles [General Cochran] gave him a shilling on condition that he should pray for King George, which he accordingly did" (*Life*, I, 431, note). His fellow student Johnston of Grange, his elder by ten years and a man of antiquarian tastes, regaled him with tales of Scotland's past when monarchs held their court in Holyrood, arousing "romantic" feelings in him. These recurred when he read William Robertson's *History of Scotland* for the first time, "which has carried me back in Imagination to the ancient days of Scottish Grandeur; has filled my mind with generous ideas of the valour of our Ancestors, and made me feel, a pleasing sympathy for the beautifule accomplished Mary" (To Grange, 13 September 1762).[8] In the same letter he speaks of "curious ideas" of the Jacobite exiles in France − "churches lighted with wax Candles, − gilded prayer Books − Prince Charles with a white feather in his hat, − Old Jacobite Ladies drinking tea in an old carved room down a north closs [close], in the month of January [the commemoration of the martyrdom of Charles I fell on 30 January]."

George Keith, tenth Earl Marischal of Scotland and Frederick the Great's adviser, had been one of the leaders of the uprisings of 1715 and 1719, and Boswell saw much of him during his visit to Berlin and Potsdam.[9] In Rome he associated with Jacobites and hobnobbed with Andrew Lumisden, secretary to the Chevalier de St. George (James VIII). And before attending a Pentecostal Mass at Frascati in May 1765, conducted by Cardinal York, Prince Charles Edward's younger brother, Boswell advised himself, in one of those memoranda through which he sought to plan the immediate future, to "think of old Scots kings, and Chapel of Holyrood".[10] By 1773, when on his Hebridean jaunt with Johnson, he expressed a clear-headed if unheroic attitude to the Stuarts in a passage not printed in this form in the published *Tour*:

> when I find how the Stuart family's right has been formed, it appears to me as but very casual and artificial. I find not the firm feudal hold for which I wish and which my imagination figures. I might fix my eye at the point of James IV, from whom my ancestor Thomas Boswell got the estate of Auchinleck, and look no further, had I a line of males from that Prince. But Queen Mary comes in the way; and I see the sons of Lennox on the throne. Besides, I consider that even supposing Prince Charles to have the right, it may be very generous for one to support another's right at every risk, but it is not wise, and I would not do it. Mr Johnson's argument of right being formed by possession and acknowledgment of the people, settles my mind, and I have now no uneasiness. With all this, he and I have a kind of *liking* for Jacobitism, something that it is not easy to define. I should guard against

it; for from what I have now put down, it is certain that my calm reasoning stops short at action, so that doing anything violent in support of the cause would only be following a sort of passion or warm whim. And talking much in favour of it may even in this secure and more liberal reign hurt a man in his rising in life. [11]

Nine years earlier, he expressed essentially the same attitude when reporting a conversation with the Earl Marischal, but without any note of calculating self-interest:

Lord Marischal dined with us at Froment's. He and I talked of Jacobitism, as how there was something pathetic and generous in it, as it was espousing the cause of a distressed and ancient royal house. My Lord however owned that they deserved to lose the throne of Britain. I own so too. I am sorry for them. I wish to forget them; and I love from my soul "Great George our King". (Journal, 22 July 1764).

Such "liking" for Jacobitism, such response to the "pathetic and generous", is in keeping with the ethos of contemporary sentimentalism — the same feelings, essentially, as can be found in varying degrees in Lady Nairne, Scott, Hogg, and dozens of historical novelists from the nineteenth century to the present day.

Boswell's libertarianism was of that aristocratic sort which is not incompatible with Toryism and which sees the freedom of small nations as best achieved under the guidance of the "natural" leaders of society: it was the liberalism of George Washington rather than Tom Paine. Though there is not much documentary evidence, it seems likely that it was rooted in childhood identification with Robert Bruce rather than with the more "democratic" Wallace. He intuitively associated the War of Independence with the baronage, as during his visit to the Magistrates' Library at Leipzig:

I saw here Anderson's *Diplomata Scotiae*. My old spirit got up, and I read them some choice passages of the Barons' letter to the Pope. They were struck with the noble sentiments of liberty of the old Scots, and they expressed their regret at the shameful Union. I felt true patriot sorrow. O infamous rascals, who sold the honour of your country to a nation against which our ancestors supported themselves with so much glory! But I say no more, only Alas, poor Scotland! (Journal, 6 October 1764).

In these moods, libertarianism and Jacobitism flowed together. And even before his visit to Corsica in 1765 another influence was added to them, though peripherally – Rousseauism, or an over-simplified version of it. In *Du Contrat Social* of two years before, Corsica had attracted Rousseau's attention:

> There is yet one country in Europe capable of legislation, and that is the island of Corsica. The valour and the constancy with which that brave people hath recovered and defended its liberty would well deserve that some wise man should teach them how to preserve it. I have some presentiment that one day that little island will astonish Europe. (Book 2, chapter 10)

There were plans for Rousseau himself to go to Corsica, write its history, and even give advice on the Corsican constitution. On his first visit to Rousseau, Boswell jokingly offered to be his "Ambassador Extraordinary" to Corsica (Journal, 15 December 1764), and he more than half expected to see the island as a proving ground for Rousseau's theories of unaccommodated man and the State of Nature.

Once in Corsica Boswell sought out General Paoli, the elected "general of the people" and leader of the islanders' struggle against Genoa and France: his experiences there strengthened an emotional identification with small nations oppressed by larger ones which in his later years was heavily overlaid by the pull of London and the anglophile's revulsion against his own countrymen. But the publication of his *Account of Corsica* (1768) and *Essays in Favour of the Brave Corsicans* (1769) makes Boswell a worthy member of that distinguished band of British writers (e.g. Byron, George Orwell, John Cornford) who have actively championed European freedom-fighters.

He could not but approve of the image projected by Paoli:

> Paoli talked very highly on preserving the independency of Corsica. "We may," said he, "have foreign powers for our friends, but they must be friends at arm's length. We may make an alliance, but we will not submit ourselves to the dominion of the greatest nation in Europe. This people who have done so much for liberty would be hewn in pieces man by man rather than allow Corsica to be sunk into the territories of another country. Some years ago, when a false rumour was spread that I had a design to yield up Corsica to the Emperor,

> a Corsican came to me and addressed me in great agitation: "What! shall the blood of so many heroes, who have sacrificed their lives for the freedom of Corsica, serve only to tinge the purple of a foreign prince!" (Journal, 22-27 October 1765)

Boswell's awe of Paoli, his investing the national leader with an aura of sublimity, was very like one strand in pre-revolutionary and indeed revolutionary French feeling — admiration for the Roman republic and the stern virtues that were imputed to the Senate and People of Rome. At his first interview he saw Paoli as an almost archetypal figure: "I found him alone, and was struck with his appearance. He is tall, strong, and well made; of a fair complexion, a sensible, free, and open countenance, and a manly and noble carriage. He was then in his fortieth year" (Journal, 21 October). The emotional pull of Rome is underlined when Boswell reports: "He observed that the Epicurean philosophy had produced but one exalted character, whereas Stoicism had been the seminary of great men" (22-27 October); but the real model for his Corsica was Sparta, and for his Paoli the legendary Lycurgus. If Paoli was the leader of guerillas and freedom-fighters, he was also a highly cultivated cosmopolitan:

> He smiled a good deal when I told him that I was much surprised to find him so amiable, accomplished, and polite; for although I knew I was to see a great man, I expected to find a rude character, an Attila King of the Goths [sic], or a Luitprand King of the Lombards' (22-27 October).

Yet Paoli's accomplishments and *politesse* were based on heroic emotion, not rationalisation.

> Paoli said, "If a man would preserve the generous glow of patriotism, he must not reason too much. Marshal Saxe reasoned, and carried the arms of France into the heart of Germany, his own country. I act from sentiment, not from reasonings."

Curiously enough, the "sentiment" which Paoli made his guide and rule, was almost identical with emotions and values central to Burns's vision:

> "Virtuous sentiments and habits," said he, "are beyond philosophical reasonings, which are not so strong, and are continually varying. If all the professors in Europe were formed

into one society, it would no doubt be a society very respectable and we should there be entertained with the best moral
lessons. Yet I believe I should find more real virtue in a
society of good peasants in some little village in the heart of
your island. (22-27 October)

At the domestic level, the humble virtues of "The Cotter's Saturday
Night" are those of Paoli's "society of good peasants", but the true
parallel is surely with the people-in-arms of "To a Haggis":

> But mark the Rustic, haggis-fed,
> The trembling earth resounds his tread,
> Clap in his walie nieve a blade,   ample fist
>   He'll mak it whissle;
> An' legs, an' arms, an' heads will sned,   cut off
>   Like taps o' thrissle.   (Stanza 7)

It was, then, in Corsica that Boswell's libertarianism came to the fore
and its qualities were defined; and it is surely not too far-fetched to
claim that heroic images, not just of the Fifteen and the Forty-five, but
also of the War of Independence, of Bruce and Wallace, played their
part in the feeling-structure of the *Journal of a Tour to Corsica*. The
deduction follows inevitably from Boswell's choice for epigraph for
the published *Corsica*, taken from the Declaration of Arbroath, the
manifesto of his beloved Scots barons: "We do not fight for glory,
wealth, or honours, but solely for that liberty without which no
virtuous man will survive."

Another instance of Boswell's ambivalent libertarianism can be seen
in his relation with John Wilkes. Boswell wrote to him on 22 April
1765: "I believe you to be a very Whig and a very Libertine. . . . I am
Dear Sir as much yours as a Scots Royalist can be", and he supported
him in the Middlesex election campaign to the extent that he believed
he had been unfairly deprived of his seat in the Commons (*Life*, II,
111-2; III, 221). But he took good care not to visit him in prison: "I
am a Scotch Laird and a Scotch Lawyer and a Scotch married man. It
would not be decent" (Journal, 20 April 1772). The electoral system
in both England and Scotland was hopelessly corrupt, and there was a
close connection between those who wanted to reform it and, in the
early stages of the Revolution at any rate, support for French democracy. In Scotland the worst abuse was what was called "nominal and
fictitious votes"; the system is too complicated to explain here.[12] Up

to the mid-eighties Boswell consistently urged their abolition, which he regarded not as "reform" but as restoration of the original electoral laws. He may have been the author of a series of letters, signed "An Old Freeholder", printed in the Edinburgh newspapers in September and October 1782, attacking the system;[13] and in 1783 he was elected preses of a meeting of the freeholders of Ayrshire to press for the abolition of nominal and fictitious votes. But in 1785, at the time of his second *Letter to the People of Scotland,* he reversed his opinions; henceforth, he was opposed to all reform of parliament, and in that year refused an invitation to be a delegate from Edinburgh to a Reform Convention.[14]

On two matters at least, Boswell's opinions were the exact opposite of Dr Johnson's: slavery, and the grievances of the American colonists. Johnson toasted the next insurrection of the negroes in the West Indies and held taxation of the colonies to be no tyranny; Boswell thought it both robbery and cruelty to "abolish a status which in all ages God has sanctioned, and man has continued", and seems to have been drawn to the Americans almost from the beginning. We do not have any record of his response to the Boston Tea Party of 16 December 1773, but when the government in retaliation closed Boston Harbour, he composed a ballad on it of the broadside sort, in which Burke's, Dempster's and Chatham's stand against the Boston Harbour Bill was celebrated in mock-heroic terms. It was published in the *London Chronicle* for 21-23 July, 1774:

> *The blade of Burke and Dempster's dirk,*
> *From Irish bog and Scottish hill,*
> *Were brandished bright, in the Court's sight,*
> *In vain against the Boston Bill . . .*

> *To the Upper House it went up souse,*   straight away
> *Of no effect was Chatham's will;*
> *His quivering crutch could hardly touch*
> *The borders of the Boston Bill . . .*

> *Come let us sing long live our King,*
> *For we are sure he means no ill,*
> *And hope the best for the oppressed*
> *By the unhappy Boston Bill.*

In the facetious column which he occasionally contributed to the *Public Advertiser* under the nom-de-plume of "Rampager", he played around with tea and its associations in the issue of 11 March 1775:

> I remember to have seen, in the Public Advertiser, a poem
> upon Tea by the Emperor of China. Had that monarch known
> that this trifling Herb had nearly embroiled the Western
> World, it would have afforded a good addition to his Verses,
> and given a kind of horrid Grandeur to the Subject. We have
> read of a *Teterrima* [most horrible] *Belli Causa;* but a sillier one
> than Tea cannot be imagined. That Scandal and little female
> Altercations have been promoted by it, is almost proverbial:
> but it is truly wonderful to find the Cause of national Ani-
> mosities, and almost of the Horrors of Slaughter and Devasta-
> tion, through a Leaf.

Four months later, on 12 August, he wrote to Temple: "I am growing
more and more an American. I see the unreasonableness of taxing
them without the consent of their Assemblies. I think our ministry are
mad in undertaking this desperate war". On 28 October the news
reached Edinburgh that a former Lord Mayor of London, the American-
born Stephen Sayre, had been arrested and charged with plotting to
seize the King's person and take possession of the Tower. That night
the Boswells were giving a small dinner party. "The news of Mr
Sayre's being committed to the Tower on a charge of high treason
agitated me. I was rather inclined to the American side of the present
grand dispute, notwithstanding Dr Johnson's eloquence; and I spoke
warmly pretty often, from the spirit of opposition principally, I
believe, as well as from a regard to what appeared to me just and
reasonable" (Journal). On 16 January 1776 he dispatched a letter to
The London Chronicle, signed "Borax", lamenting Scottish apathy
towards the American war (Journal), while in the Rampager of 9
March, couched fantastically in bird imagery, he introduced the
American question towards the end of his column:

> Many a *Raven* is now croaking destruction to Great Britain,
> unless she will fly from her own Grove, invite the assistance of
> foreign Birds, and crush her vigorous Offspring on the other side
> of the Atlantic: But I much fear that we are egregiously mis-
> taken, that our Offspring are too numerous and too well fledged
> to be reduced to *infantine Dependence* on their Mother, which
> Nature never intended, and which is really not desirable for the
> Mother. . . . Sincerely do I wish to see the *Dove,* with the Olive
> Branch; and when Ambassadors of Conciliation are sent out I
> shall sing with the young 'Squire in Dr Goldsmith's Comedy,

> *But of all the Birds in the Air,*
> *There is none like the three jolly Pigeons.* (*She Stoops to Conquer* Act I)

Boswell wrote other feebly satiric Rampagers poking fun at the British rôle in the American war on 27 August 1777 and 14 August 1779, which add to the evidence that he never wavered in his pro-colonial stance while the war was on. For serious comment we must go to letters and Journal. For example, "The town was illuminated on account of the news of a victory in Georgia over Count d'Estaing and the Americans. It gave me no pleasure, for I considered that it would only encourage a longer continuance of the ruinous war" (Journal, 25 December 1779). Or again, "Restrained my joy on Lord Cornwallis's surrender, not to give offence. But it inspirited me" (Journal, 1 December 1781). And on 7 February 1782 he entertained Lords Eglinton and Kellie, Lady Colville and Lady Anne Erskine to dinner despite the fact that the King and Privy Council had proclaimed a public fast and humiliation for the British defeat. "We had an excellent dinner, choice wines, and the best company" (Journal). Yet once hostilities ceased and provisional articles of peace were concluded acknowledging the colonies as "free and independent states", Boswell's royalism came to the fore: "was truly hurt that my sovereign should be so humiliated" (Journal, 9 December 1782).

3. *Burns to* 1789

For Burns, the crucial years between the ages of thirteen and eighteen were spent, not at university with the sons of lawyers, lairds and merchants, but on the stony unprofitable fields of Mount Oliphant farm, near Ayr. There, his brother Gilbert tells us, Robert "at the age of thirteen, assisted in thrashing the crop of corn, and at fifteen was the principal labourer on the farm". Although life was more comfortable when his father took on the tenancy of Lochlea in Tarbolton parish in Robert's nineteenth year, he never forgot the hardships of Mount Oliphant; the family's experiences there laid the foundations for his life long hatred of oppression and exploitation.[15] An early song, "A Ruined Farmer", with the refrain line "And its O fickle Fortune, O!", seems clearly based on his father's condition at this time. It was personal experience of poverty, and what he had seen of others reduced to beggary and despair, that lay behind the picture of the poor farmer condemned to "thole a factor's snash" in "The Twa Dogs", and his own real fear of destitution, however cavalierly treated, in the "Epistle to Davie, a Brother Poet":

> "Mair spier na, nor fear na,"
> Auld age ne'er mind a feg:
> The last o't, the warst o't,
> Is only but to beg.

> To lie in kilns and barns at e'en,
> When banes are craz'd, and bluid is thin,
> Is, doubtless, great distress!
> Yet then content could make us blest . . .
> Nae mair then, we'll care then,
> Nae farther can we fa'.   (lines 25-32, 41-42)

And his memories of the plight of a relative of his mother's inspired "Man was made to Mourn". Writing to Mrs Dunlop on 16 August 1788, Burns mentions an old grand-uncle who had gone blind, and whose "most voluptuous enjoyment was to sit down & cry while my Mother would sing the simple old song of, *The Life & Age of Man*". The song began thus:

> 'Twas in the sixteenth-hunder year
> Of God and fifty-three
> Frae Christ was born, that bought us dear,
> As writings testifie:

> On January the sixteenth day,
> As I did lie alone,
> With many a sob and sigh did say,
> Ah! man was made to moan![16]

According to Gilbert Burns,

> He [Robert] used to remark to me, that he could not well conceive a more mortifying picture of human life than a man seeking work. In casting about in his mind how this sentiment might be brought forward, the elegy *Man was made to Mourn* was composed.[17]

It is out of such materials, then, that the poem is made — recollections of a suffering grand-uncle, his own miseries, and the tribulations of practically the whole population of Ayrshire in the difficult years 1781-4.

During his seventeenth year Burns spent some weeks at Kirkoswald with his mother's brother, learning "Mensuration, Surveying, and Dialling &c" at the local school. He met dissipated smugglers there, and perhaps (it was the summer of 1775) seamen who had voyaged across the Atlantic, bringing tidings of revolutionary developments in America. Though the politics that came home most insistently to Burns during these years, and indeed right up to 1784, when he would be twenty-five, were ecclesiastical and doctrinal, he cannot but have heard of the Declaration of Independence and followed, perhaps a month or two after they were reported in the newspapers, all the developments up to the surrender at Yorktown and the Peace of 1783, which reduced the soldier's doxy in "The Jolly Beggars" to "beg in despair". Events in America, too, must surely have been discussed by the Tarbolton Bachelors' Club which Burns helped to found in 1780, before or after the more formal topics which were debated.

One trait that Burns shares with Boswell, Jacobite sentiment and a regard for the Earls Marischal, can be traced to what he learned in childhood of his family history; indeed, he says that it was his father's loyalty to the Keiths that impelled him to emigrate from Kincardineshire:

> My Fathers rented land of the noble Kieths of Marshal, and had the honor to share their fate. − I do not use the word, Honor, with any reference to Political principles; loyal and disloyal I take to be merely relative terms in that ancient and formidable court known in this Country by the name of CLUB-LAW. − Those who dare welcome Ruin and shake hands with Infamy for what they sincerely believe to be the cause of their God or their King − "Brutus and Cassius are honorable men". − I mention this circumstance because it threw my father on the world at large. . . . (To Dr John Moore, 2 August 1787)

By 1789 Burns had inflated these feelings into heroic myth:

> But with your Ladyship I have the honor to be conected by one of the strongest & most endearing ties in the whole Moral World − Common Sufferers in a Cause where even to be unfortunate is glorious, the Cause of Heroic Loyalty! − Though my Fathers had not illustrious Honors and vast properties to hazard in the contest; though they left their humble cottages only to add so many units more to the

unnoted croud that followed their Leaders; yet, what they
could they did, and what they had they lost: with unshaken
firmness and unconcealed Political Attachments, they shook
hands with Ruin for what they esteemed the cause of their
King and their Country. (To Lady Winifred Maxwell Con-
stable, 16 December 1789)

Burns's recorded responses to the American Revolution are retrospective, and more consistent with his attitude to the French Revolution than are Boswell's. The earliest is a fragmentary ballad of the
broadside type, "When Guilford good" which was printed in the
Edinburgh Edition of 1787 though it may have been written as early
as 1784. The statesmen of the time are sometimes referred to by
subsidiary titles or the names of obscure estates; thus Lord North
becomes 'Guilford good' and Lord George Germain appears as 'Sackville'. "Such deviousness was one of the conventions of that kind of
popular satire," although it is not allowed to dominate the poem. To
have disguised Rockingham, Burgoyne, Dundas and Fox beyond all
recognition would have destroyed the poem's character as a political
comedy that could be enjoyed by ordinary people.

Here is how, in the first stanza, Burns handles the Boston Tea Party
and the beginnings of the American Revolution:

> When Guilford good our pilot stood,
>   An' did our hellim thraw, man;   helm   turn
> Ae night, at tea, began a plea,
>   Within Americà, man:
>
> Then up they gat the maskin-pat,   tea-pot
>   And in the sea did jaw, man: dash
> An' did nae less, in full Congress,
>   Than quite refuse our law, man.   (lines 1-8)

In the seventh stanza, Fox's short-lived political victory in 1783 and
the collapse of his ministry after the defeat of his famous India Bill are
described with equal contempt, this time in terms of a game of cards:

> Then clubs an' hearts were Charlie's cartes:
> He swept the stakes awa', man,
> Till the diamond's ace, of Indian race,
> Led him a sair faux pas, man . . .   (lines 41-52)

In the fifth stanza, when "Charlie" Fox speaks against North's *régime* he loosens his "tinkler jaw" almost as if he were one of the Jolly Beggars; in the ninth, both he and North are likened to homely golfers, and "Willie" Pitt to their ball. British generalship is treated with the utmost derision, while Westminster political combinations are likened to the moves in a childish game that farmers and ploughmen, poor, voteless creatures though they may be, just cannot take seriously.

Burns's next poetical response to American events, the "Address of Beelzebub", is a much more root and branch affair. It is a superbly mordant satire which manages to unite indignation at the sufferings of the poor, his concern in "Man was Made to Mourn", with enthusiasm for American "liberty". Another of its themes is Highland emigration — not as the result of forced clearances, but as voluntary escape from poverty. At a meeting of the "gentlemen of the Highland Society", as reported by the *Edinburgh Advertiser* for 30 May 1786, the Earl of Breadalbane stated:

> that five hundred persons had agreed to emigrate from the estates of M'Donald of Glengary; that they had subscribed money, purchased ships, &c., to carry their design into effect. The noblemen and gentlemen agreed to co-operate with government to frustrate their design; and to recommend to the principal noblemen and gentlemen in the Highlands to endeavour to prevent emigration, by improving the fisheries, agriculture, and manufactures, and particularly to enter into a subscription for that purpose.

Burns does not appear to have been over-impressed by these long-term schemes for the establishment of a balanced economy. What interested him were the immediate sufferings of the Highlanders, in particular the news that "the noblemen and gentlemen" intended to "co-operate with government" in order to keep their tenants on the land. The note of indignation is apparent even in the wording of the epigraph:

> To the Right Honorable the Earl of Breadalbane, President of the Right Honorable the Highland Society, which met on the 23rd of May last, at the *Shakespeare,* Covent Garden, to concert ways and means to frustrate the designs of five hundred Highlanders who . . . were so audacious as to attempt an escape from their lawful lords and masters whose property they were, by emigrating . . . to the wilds of Canada, in search of that fantastic thing — Liberty.

Among twentieth-century Scottish novelists such as Neil Gunn and "Fionn MacColla" it has become conventional to represent the typical Highland laird as a wicked oppressor who forced his clansmen to emigrate. But here is Burns criticising the aristocracy for doing the very opposite — for trying to *prevent* the flight from the glens and isles.

What justifies the lairds' forcible restraint of their tenantry is the terrible possibility that they might follow the example of the colonists:

> *Then up amang thae lakes and seas,*
> *They'll mak what rules and laws they please* . . .   (lines 11-12)

If that were to happen, they might produce their own revolutionary leaders, men as daring as Hancock, Franklin, Washington, or Montgomerie. Once rid of such wise and experienced leaders as North and Sackville, the rabble might even "to Patrician rights aspire" — no landowner could ever contemplate such a happening with equanimity. The sonorous list of these great American names adds an extra dimension to the poem, which is still further enriched by the delicious irony of the four succeeding lines:

> *An' whare will ye get Howes and Clintons*
> *To bring them to a right repentance?*
> *To cowe the rebel generation,*
> *An' save the honor o' the nation?*   (lines 23-6)

The point is, of course, that Howe and Clinton, for all their gallantry, did not in the end defeat the rebels; consequently, they cannot have saved the honour of the nation, except in so far as they fought bravely. The Highland gentry would be even less capable of defeating their migrated tenants than the British government had been some five to ten years previously, for they would lack even such partially successful generals as those who defeated Washington at White Plains and Brandywine, or secured the capture of Charleston — perhaps, indeed, the lairds are now so degenerate that they can no longer produce good military leaders. It follows that the suppression of their former "property" would bring them even less glory than the British got from the American Revolution.

There are few lines in English poetry which express so violent a hatred of a ruling class as the next four, in which Beelzebub apostrophises Breadalbane as follows:

> *They, an' be damn'd! what right hae they*
> *To meat or sleep or light o' day,*
> *Far less to riches, pow'r, or freedom,*
> *But what your lordship likes to gie them?* (lines 27-30)

Turning to Glengarry, Beelzebub urges the Highland lairds to be even more ruthless towards their tenants than they are at present. To rob them and impound their goods is not enough to cow their stubborn spirit; nothing less than punitive expeditions will suffice:

> *But smash them! crush them a' to spails,*   chips
> *An' rot the dyvors i' the jails!*   bankrupts
> *The young dogs, swinge them to the labour:*
> *Let wark an' hunger mak them sober!*
> *The hizzies, if they're aughtlins fawsont,* at all good-looking
> *Let them in Drury Lane be lesson'd!*
> *An' if the wives an' dirty brats*
> *Come thiggin at your doors an' yetts,* begging; gates
> *Flaffin wi' duds an' grey wi' beas',* flapping with rags; vermin
> *Frightin awa your deuks an' geese,* ducks
> *Get out a horsewhip or a jowler,* bulldog
> *The langest thong, the fiercest growler,*
> *An' gar the tatter'd gypsies pack* make
> *Wi' a' their bastards on their back!* (lines 39-52)

If Glengarry follows this advice, he will deserve one of the best places in Hell, where, indeed, Beelzebub longs to meet him; he will be given the innermost corner next the fire, cheek-by-jowl with the great tyrants of history:

> *'Tween Herod's hip an' Polycrate.*
> *Or (if you on your station tarrow)* hesitate
> *Between Almagro and Pizarro . . .* (lines 58-60)

"The Address of Beelzebub" looks forward to the mood of the early seventeen-nineties. It may not be politically or historically accurate; it may do less than justice to the Highland Society; but in its championship of freedom from constraint and its passionate hatred of control by landlords it is as near the French spirit as anything else produced by Burns at this period.

In a remarkable letter in the *Edinburgh Evening Courant.* 22 November 1788, under the nom-de-plume of "A Briton", Burns cogently states his political position in the year before the outbreak of the

French Revolution. The occasion was the sermon of his parish minister for the centenary of the Glorious Revolution of 1688:

> I went last Wednesday to my parish church, most cordially to join in grateful acknowledgements to the Author of all Good, for the consequent blessings of the Glorious Revolution. To that auspicious event we owe no less than our liberties religious and civil — to it we are likewise indebted for the present Royal Family, the ruling features of whose administration have ever been, mildness to the subject, and tenderness of his rights. Bred and educated in revolution principles, the principles of reason and common sense, it could not be any silly political prejudice that made my heart revolt at the harsh abusive manner in which the Reverend Gentleman mentioned the House of Stuart, and which, I am afraid, was too much the language of that day. We may rejoice sufficiently in our deliverance from past evils, without cruelly raking up the ashes of those whose misfortune it was, perhaps, as much as their crimes, to be the authors of those evils; and may bless God for all his goodness to us as a nation, without, at the same time, cursing a few ruined powerless exiles, who only harboured ideas, and made attempts, that most of us would have done, had we been in their situation.
>
> "The bloody and tyrannical house of Stuart" may be said with propriety and justice, when compared with the present Royal Family, and the liberal sentiments of our days. But is there no allowance to be made for the manners of the times? Were the royal contemporaries of the Stuarts more mildly attentive to the rights of man? Might not the epithets of "bloody and tyrannical" be with at least equal justice applied to the house of Tudor, of York, or any other of their predecessors? . . .
>
> The Stuarts have been condemned and laughed at for the folly and impracticability of their attempts, in 1715 and 1745. That they failed, I bless my God most fervently; but cannot join in the ridicule against them. Who does not know that the abilities or defects of leaders and commanders are often hidden until put to the touchstone of exigence; and that there is a caprice of fortune, an omnipotence in particular accidents, and conjunctures of circumstances, which exalt us

as heroes, or brand us as madmen, just as they are for or against us?

Man, Mr Printer, is a strange, weak, inconsistent being — Who would believe, Sir, that in this our Augustan age of liberality and refinement, while we seem so justly sensible and jealous of our rights and liberties, and animated with such indignation against the very memory of those who would have subverted them, who would suppose that a certain people, under our national protection, should complain, not against a Monarch and a few favourite advisers, but against our whole legislative body, of the very same imposition and oppression . . . and almost in the very same terms as our forefathers did against the family of Stuart! I will not, I cannot, enter into the merits of the cause; but I dare say, the American Congress, in 1776, will be allowed to have been as able and as enlightened, and, a whole empire will say, as honest, as the English Convention in 1688; and that the fourth of July will be as sacred to their posterity as the fifth of November is to us.

The letter unites his theology (Man is born good, not evil, but is "a strange, weak inconsistent being"), his feelings for the oppressed and the victims of man's inhumanity to man, his sentimental Jacobitism, and his recognition of the positive aspects of the Revolution settlement and the Hanoverian succession. He made the same point in a more unbuttoned and vigorous manner in a letter of 13 November to Mrs Dunlop. The theology is absent, however, and there is a savagery in his ironical criticism of the Hanoverians that is understandably missing from a text intended for a newspaper:

Is it not remarkable, odiously remarkable, that tho' manners are more civilized, & the rights of mankind better understood, by an Augustan Century's improvement, yet in this very reign of heavenly Hanoverianism, & almost in this very year, an empire beyond the Atlantic has had its REVOLUTION too, & for the very same maladministration & legislative misdemeanors in the illustrious & sapientipotent Family of H — as was complained of in the "tyranical & bloody house of STUART".

4. *Common Humanity*

Despite his political and social Toryism and his self-identification with the ruling élite, Boswell again and again came to the aid of individual victims of injustice. One of his most endearing traits was an ability to strike an immediate rapport with persons casually met, whether they came from his own class or "the lower orders", though often it led to his dignity being punctured, both in his own eyes and those of his inferiors. There were glaring contradictions even here, as in his youthful dealings with Jacob Hänni, the Swiss who was his servant for much of Grand Tour. He switched inconsistently between authoritarian reserve and genial familiarity; interfered unnecessarily in matters which should have been Jacob's sole concern; and − a trait which often irritated Dr Johnson − kept bombarding him with questions. As he wrote after a tête-à-tête during which Jacob complained "that it was impossible for servants to live with me, as I was not, like other gentlemen, content with external acquiescence, but would always show them clearly that they were wrong":

> I am always studying human nature and making experiments on the lowest characters, so that I am too much in the secret with regard to the weakness of man in reality, and my honest, impetuous disposition cannot take up with that eternal repetition of fictitious minutiae by which unthinking men of fashion preserve a great distinction between master and servant. By having Jacob so free with me, I have felt as servants do, and been convinced that the greatest part of them laugh in their sleeve very heartily at the parade of their lords, knowing well that eating, drinking, sleeping, and other offices of nature are common to all. (Journal, 17 December 1765)

Boswell's sympathy for harassed individuals is most obvious in his dealings with the criminals he defended in the courts: he felt more deeply when a poor man was executed than if the victim were rich. "Why it is, I know not, but we compassionate less a genteel man" (Notes for Journal, 11 February 1767). And one must agree with Frederick Pottle that perhaps the most moving section of the whole Boswell archive is a bale of papers relating to legal clients of his who were tried for their lives, and hanged (most of them) in spite of all his efforts.[18] His emotional response sometimes bordered on the morbid. He was irresistibly drawn to public hangings, which he attended whenever he could, often thrusting his company on the condemned in their cells the night before their execution. As with Jacob Hänni, he wanted to know everything to the very bottom, and plied them with questions: how afraid were they, what were their precise regrets at leaving this vale of tears, did they repent? Another sort of "experiment on the lowest characters" is shown in his frequent recourse to prostitutes, not every one of whom was "a whore worthy of Boswell", or as delightfully uninhibited as Sally Forrester,[19] Jeany Wells,[20] or the "fine lass" who was a natural daughter of Lord Kinnaird. The first time they met, he stayed with her for an hour and a half in a close in the Luckenbooths "and was most amorous. . . . I was so happy with Jeanie Kinnaird that I very philosophically reasoned that there was to me so much virtue mixed with licentious love that perhaps I might be privileged. For it made me humane, polite, generous" (Journal, 19 January 1768). Perhaps the majority were never seen as human beings — mere objects, enjoyed in exhilaration or disgust, then forgotten until the inevitable symptoms appeared. Yet sometimes, as with those condemned to die, there was a genuine attempt to realise the girl as a person, to sympathise, and even to help.

The best known instance of Boswell's humanity towards a woman of the people is his campaign on behalf of "the girl from Botany Bay", which occurred during the revolutionary years themselves, at the very time when politically he was most opposed to the men and the principles of the Revolution. She was Mary Broad, transported for stealing a cloak, who escaped from the penal colony at the end of March 1791 with her husband, two small children, and seven other convicts. They sailed the three thousand miles to Timor in an open boat; all survived the journey despite attacks by aborigines when they put ashore for water and repairs. Alas, they were arrested in Timor and returned to England in a ship belonging to the East India Company, along with the *Bounty* mutineers. Mary's husband and children and three of their convict companions died on the voyage home. In July 1792 she and the other survivors were committed to Newgate, whereupon Boswell mounted a spirited campaign to save her. He appealed to Dundas and others in the government for a pardon, which was finally granted in May 1793, and collected seventeen guineas in a subscription for her. On hearing that her father had inherited a huge legacy, Boswell encouraged her to seek out her relations in Cornwall;

when the story proved false he settled an annuity of ten pounds on her.[21] Boswell had also petitioned for the release of the other surviving convicts; when they were set at liberty at the beginning of November, all four called round to see him, but he was unfortunately out (Journal, 2 November 1793).

It is clear that Boswell's treatment of the poor and the dependent was as full of contradictions as his behaviour in other respects. His "familiarity" with the like of Jacob Hänni, his sympathy for criminals who were not genteel, his compassion for some prostitutes, and his active philanthropy towards persons in distress like Mary Broad, were in keeping with the general tenor of eighteenth century sentimentalism, which was itself the source of revolutionary feelings and ideas. But at the same time, on his own estate of Auchinleck, his benevolence was much more that of a feudal proprietor towards his dependents. He was particularly concerned in the seventeen-nineties (he was, of course, an absentee landlord) that the tenantry should pay their rents punctually, and in extreme cases he was even willing that they should be turned off their holdings. He wrote to his overseer Andrew Gibb on 4 June 1791 that no-one "upon my estate has reason to fear that I will be a hard master", and went on in the same letter to give what he no doubt regarded as humanely firm instructions:

> As to George Paton, I am sorry to see him falling back so. He has a cautioner [surety] for five years rents and if he does not pay up equally with the rest, I mean his Whitsunday money rent and Candlemas meal, let him be proceeded against, and if he fails to pay, proceed against his cautioner. But do not deal harder with him than with the others; I mean let his Martinmas rent remain unpaid till I come home in August.
>
> Let me add as to Andrew Arnot, that if he suffers his cattle to trespass, and if there be an appearance of much debt to others besides me, his stock and crop should be secured for my behoof.

It was the actions of more hard-hearted landlords than Boswell, or rather of their agents, towards people like Andrew Arnot that gave rise to Burns's most moving expressions of pre-revolutionary sentiment — his indignation at the oppression of the Highland tenantry in the "Address of Beelzebub", the misery of the "poor o'er-laboured wight" in "Man was made to mourn", or the distress of the "tenant-bodies, scant o' cash" in "The Twa Dogs" as they "thole a factor's snash" (lines 95-6):

> There's monie a creditable stock
> O' decent, honest, fawsont folk,   well-doing
> Are riven out baith root an' branch,   torn
> Some rascal's pridefu' greed to quench   (lines 141-4).

But it is "To a Mouse" that comes closest to the worst that could befall tenants in Auchinleck:

> Now thou's turn'd out, for a' thy trouble,
> But house or hald,   without
> To thole the Winter's sleety dribble,   endure
> An' cranreuch cauld!   (lines 33-6)   hoar-frost

Burns's choice of the word "hald" [holding, property held] makes his humanised mouse a symbol of the poor peasant everywhere, and the "cruel coulter" is his equivalent of Blake's "dark Satanic mills" — the keen edge of the ploughshare of social change that breaks down the houses of both Lowland and Highland cotters.

The celebration of common humanity at other levels, those of empathy with ordinary men and women in lyric or comic context, is surely the feature in which Burns excels all the other British poets of the revolutionary era. It is seen in songs like "Last May a braw wooer", "Ay waukin O", and "What can a young lassie dae wi' an auld man", where the protagonist is a young girl in love or tiptoeing her way through the marriage market. It is seen in the many pieces where he hymns the values of male companionship and brotherhood — ordinary *fraternité* free from any idealistic aura except an occasional tinge of rather homespun freemasonry. And it is seen above all in the anarchic companionship of the beggars in "Love and Liberty" ("The Jolly Beggars"), written some four years before the fall of the Bastille. The final chorus is a rousing satiric critique of the values of civil and indeed aristocratic society:

> See the smoking bowl before us!
> Mark our jovial, ragged ring!
> Round and round take up the chorus,
> And in raptures let us sing:

Chorus: *A fig for those by law protected*
     Liberty's a glorious feast!
  Courts for cowards were erected,
     Churches built to please the priest.

What is title, what is treasure,
  What is reputation's care?
If we lead a life of pleasure,
  'Tis no matter how or where.

With the ready trick and fable
  Round we wander all the day:
And at night, in barn or stable,
  Hug our doxies on the hay.

Does the train-attended carriage
  Thro' the country lighter rove?
Does the sober bed of marriage
  Witness brighter scenes of love?

Life is all a variorum,
  We regard not how it goes:
Let them cant about decorum,
  Who have character to lose.

Here's to budgets, bags and wallets!
  Here's to all the wandering train!
Here's our ragged brats and callets!
  One and all cry out, Amen!

Chorus: *A fig for those by law protected*
     Liberty's a glorious feast!
  Courts for cowards were erected,
     Churches built to please the priest.

There is more than a hint here of the great things coming on in Britain and in Europe.

5. *Boswell* 1789-1795

We have no record of Boswell's reaction to the fall of the Bastille on the fourteenth of July 1789, but we do have an early response from his correspondent William Johnson Temple on 24 August combining an almost Wordsworthian delight at the turn of events with distress at the violence which had already begun to occur. (It had been reported in the press that some three hundred persons had been killed and wounded at the taking of the Bastille, and that "after a short trial" the Governor, the Fort Major, and other officers were executed by first shooting them and then cutting off their heads; and no doubt some news of events in the countryside, the "grande peur" of the second half of July, and the burning of the châteaux, had begun to percolate across the Channel.)[22] Temple – Boswell's "oldest and most intimate friend", and at this time vicar of St. Gluvias at Penryn in Cornwall – put it this way:

> The light that has lately beamed upon France is astonishing. Did it diffuse itself from America, or from the sentiments of their late writers? It is to be lamented that revolutions so favourable to human kind are so frequently attended with scenes of horror: but it is the same in the natural or material world & individuals are as little spared. After Storms & Tempest, Inundations & Earthquakes the Sun shines again with brighter splendor & perhaps all the Powers of Nature acquire new force & vigour. Yet why must Evils *be,* to produce Good? Say what we will, *This* will ever puzzle Philosophy. (MS Yale C 2875)

Boswell's first surviving comment, in a letter to Temple of 28 November, shows him at this still early stage already a fierce opponent of the Revolution. It was written after the French royal family had been forcibly removed from Versailles to Paris, and after the confiscation of all church property on 2 November. But even before this, newspapers and periodicals had been reporting "the unexampled violences every where committed in this country", and citing events like the savage butchery of such aristocrats as Mm. Cureau and Monbesson who, it was said, had their noses and ears cut off before being beheaded.[23] Immediately before his comment, Boswell had used the word "liberal", which by a somewhat Sternian association of ideas led him on to:

> That venerable sound brings to my mind the ruffians in France who are attempting to destroy all order ecclesiastical and civil. The present state of that country is an intellectual earthquake, a whirlwind, a mad insurrection without any immediate cause, and therefore we see to what a horrible anarchy it tends. I do not mean that the French ought not to have a *Habeas Corpus* Act. But I know nothing more they wanted.

Temple did not reply till 21 February 1790, in a mildly reasonable tone:

> The troubles in France are indeed dreadful; but may not order & security arise out of anarchy & alarm, & we must recollect that no government was ever greatly improved without previous compulsion. Every one confesses that the People in France were in general exposed to great arrogance & oppression. (MS Yale C 2880)

By 18 October 1790 Temple was waxing enthusiastic over his friend Sir Christopher Hawkins's impressions of Paris:

> Hawkins was a month at Paris & heard the Debates in the National Assembly. They have not a Pitt or a Fox but many excellent speakers. All the country seemed quiet & the assembly in high veneration. A brother of Mr Gwatkin called on me this morning, who was present at the grand affair in the field of Mars [where, on the first anniversary of the Fall of the Bastille, the Constituent Assembly had organised a spectacular Festival of the Federation in an atmosphere of "joyous reconciliation".] He had no idea of a scene so magnificent so striking. Surely this revolution is one of the most astonishing events in history. Almost without bloodshed or tumult, a nation of slaves for ages are almost unanimous in one day as it were in the cause of freedom. Whatever men value & hold dear, rank, privilege, property are enthusiastically offered on the altar of Liberty. All Burke's sophistry will never prevent me from thinking there was something very bad in a government that all ranks of men [see]med eager to overturn from its [fo]undations. (MS Yale C 2892)

Unfortunately Boswell's replies to these letters are missing, but we learn of Temple's conversion to the anti-revolutionary position in his letter of 17 December, immediately after reading Burke's *Reflections*, which were published on 1 November (MS Yale C 2896).

Boswell's most arresting response to the Revolution is in the form of sketch-plans for a tragedy, to be entitled *Favras*.[24] Thomas de Mahy, Marquis de Favras, was arrested on 24 December 1789 and charged with plotting to assassinate Bailly, the Mayor of Paris, and the statesmen Necker and Lafayette; to remove the King and Queen from the Tuileries and get them out of the country, only to have them return later in the train of a foreign army. Most historians think that Favras was "set up" by agents provocateurs with the aim of destroying "Monsieur", the King's brother, who was supposed to be behind the conspiracy. During the legal process, which lasted until 17 February 1790, Favras stoutly protested his innocence and nobly refused to save his life by implicating Monsieur.[25] At midnight on the eighteenth he was sentenced "to make the *amende honorable* before the principal gate of the cathedral of Nôtre Dame — to be afterwards conducted by the executioner in a cart to the Place de Grêve, with his head and feet naked, holding in his hand a lighted flambeau of two pounds weight, and clothed in a linen frock, covered with brimstone, having a label on his breast and his back, with this inscription — "Conspirator against the State". Continuing its report of his execution on the nineteenth, *The Gentleman's Magazine* seems to rely without any irony on an official French account:

> The concourse of people that flocked together to witness the humiliation and punishment of the first judicial victim to the liberties of France was immense. But, notwithstanding his crimes, neither excess nor exultation tarnished the execution of the law. The tears which were not refused even to suffering guilt proved how little a mild and generous nation merited the epithets of "a bloody and ferocious democracy".[26]

One cannot even call *Favras* an unfinished drama, because all that survive are some MS fragments of Boswell's plan, in places difficult to interpret, and one or two puffs about his intentions in the public press. Taken together, these give us a fair notion of the play as it existed in his mind. The principal conflict is ideological:

> The Play opens at the time when the Tiers Etat are sitting & the King has made all fair concessions. Favras & Dumont his

> intimate friend from his youth come on & talk of publick
> measures being on opposite sides. Dumont has served in
> America with La Fayette & is full of democratical sentiments,
> Favras has served in the french army in the War in Germany
> has had honours & distinctions from his Sovereign is highly
> monarchical & in Lord Thurlow's words exclaims when I
> forget him may God forget me.

The summary continues:

> Dumont who has his head full of the fiery modern writings
> about the rights of men raves like Rousseau. Favras calmly &
> firmly argues against this shewing that there *are no* rights
> ridicules Lord Lansdownes rhodomontade the people have all
> rights & Kings have none. Shews that subordination & right
> of any sort are coeval and co-existent. Admits that there have
> been faults but maintains they are now sufficiently remedied.
> Dumont is eager for more concessions.

The summary now becomes somewhat elliptical, though it is clear
that Boswell intended to bring his pro-Stuart sentiment for the "Royal
Martyr" into the balance against revolutionary ideas:

> Favras says it is cowardly & ungenerous . . . of them . . .
> mentions that in a neighbouring isle that wondrous is . . .
> rivals even their great monarchy. Charles the First of that
> unhappy Stuart Race (pay some compliment pathetically)
> Dumont intreats that he may at least be quiet & not render
> himself obnoxious to the National Assembly. He *will* not be
> prudent. Arraigns that as a sneaking quality when great
> duties require bold exertion. Was this or that (naming great
> men) prudent. . . .

The manuscript in the Yale Boswell Collection containing the above
summary also includes a separate fragment about Boswell's intentions,
stating that the play is to be written with Kemble in mind for the
principal part:

> They say a Play Wright I am a Play Taylor. I shall fit the part
> on my friend Jack [Kemble] by & by. I shall cut it or
> embroider it for him. The liberality of Mr Sheridan in admit-
> ting upon his boards, a Play which abounds in sentiments the
> reverse of his upon the Revolution in France.

There follows a sentence which elevates Boswell's fascination with conflicting ideas and emotions into a statement of artistic principle that looks forward to Scott's treatment of opposing extremes in the Waverley Novels a generation later: "The Theatre should not be clogged with politicks but exhibit one day *The Regicide* and another *Charles the First."* The difference of course is that Scott set such opposites against each other in a single work, whereas Boswell is envisaging tolerant spectators attending plays of different persuasions on successive nights.

In this second fragment Boswell next turns to the character of Favras, who seems almost like the expansion of a Jacobite ideal, and then to what he clearly intends as a key image in the symbolism of the play:

> Favras's character as a faithful loyalist with the high spirit both of *Noblesse* and the Soldier will be admirably delineated. His image of the *fleur de-lys* of France being only in decay for a season to revive with fresh lustre in all its glory like the lilly of the field is particularly beautiful.

The summary breaks off abruptly, and with a gap at the beginning of the sentence:

> And my last accents shall be . . . will inbound from the bosoms of generous Britons who adore their Monarch & are sensible of the blessings of our happy constitution and. . . .

These hints are enough to show that *Favras*, as it existed in Boswell's mind, involved the sublimation of political emotions that had dominated him for many years. He had long run together retrospective feelings of Jacobite loyalty with the adoration of "Great George our King": now the heroism of a royalist judicial martyr in France was to be linked to both sorts of *British* loyalty in a paean of praise to the constitution that had developed from the Glorious Revolution of 1688.

In his puffing article in *The Public Advertiser* of 24 March, Boswell indicated that the fourth act would end with "God Save the King", and that "The acclamation of the audience at this loyal conclusion will, however, be matter of *serious joy*" and "will keep all in glow for the fifth act". He also inserted in the very same number of *The Public Advertiser* some McGonagalesque doggerel which boisterously put himself on a par with Burke, whose forthcoming work was of course on a much larger scale than is indicated here:

On Hearing that Mr Burke is bringing out a pamphlet and
Boswell a Tragedy, both against the Revolution in France

> *Sure Britain's Isle will seem prodigious fierce,*
> *Burke in wild prose, and Boswell in wild verse.*
> *Burke's blank verse prose the Tory flame will wake*
> *And Boswell's boisterous verse make Frenchmen quake.*
> *Thanks to the gods! Old England's sons are clear,*
> *'Tis Teague and Sawney who will thus appear.*

The rhythm and phrasing of the first line show that Boswell had an
Irish tune and Irish accents in mind, while the last couplet plays with
the image of a stage Irishman and a stage Scotsman saving the *English!*

A more substantial work from the revolutionary years was the poem
No Abolition of Slavery, or, the Universal Empire of Love, which Boswell
published anonymously on 16 April 1791. Its three hundred octo-
syllabics are what MacDiarmid might have called an extraordinary
clamjamfrey, mixing satire against the abolitionists with sentimental
courtly love. The two glaring opposites out of which it is made are
starkly set against each other in the hackneyed quotations on the
title-page:

> Facit indignatio versis.   HORAT
> Omnia vincit amor.   OVID

Most of the first half of this 300-line poem is given over to "indignatio"
against those "Noodles" who rave for reversal of the "African's
improv'd condition", and particularly the statesmen, the "Slaves of
Power". Naturally, Wilberforce comes first:

> *Go, W.... with narrow scull,*
> *Go home, and preach away at Hull . . .*
> *I hate your little wittling sneer,*
> *Your pert and self-sufficient leer.*   (lines 25-6, 29-30)

He jibes at Windham (who was to become Secretary for War under
Pitt in 1794) in terms reminiscent of Mrs Thatcher scorning the Wets:
he is "with the whining tribe", and quite effeminate in his opposition
to the trade:

> *Shalt THOU, a Roman free and rough,*
> *Descend to weak blue stocking stuff,*
> *And cherish feelings soft and kind,*
> *Till you emasculate your mind.*   (lines 83-6)

Lines 87-92 are on Courtenay – not merely an abolitionist and supporter of the Revolution, but irreligious to boot ("On sceptic themes he wildly raves", line 90). Then, sadly, he turns to Burke:

> *BURKE, art THOU here too? thou, whose pen*
> *Could blast the fancied rights of men:*
> *Pray, by what logick are those rights*
> *Allow'd to Blacks – deny'd to Whites?*

Charles James Fox is "Faction's chief Antistes" who, "more than Samson Agonistes" would "pull down/Our charter'd rights, our church, our crown" (lines 97-100), and to his sorrow Pitt is also an abolitionist, though quite possibly not from principle but from political expediency in order to set lesser men quarrelling about inessentials while he safely steers the ship of state on its appointed course (lines 135-8).

When he turns from personalities to arguments, Boswell is quite clear that the abolitionists are in the same ideological camp as the revolutionaries across the Channel. The Rights of Man lead to democracy, political chaos, and the destruction of the entire social order, whose bases are property and subordination. Any attack on slavery is an attack on property, and therefore on subordination. Black slaves share in the blessings of civilisation precisely *because* they are subordinate to their masters:

> *Slavery, subjection, what you will,*
> *Have ever been, and will be still:*
> *Trust me, that in this world of woe*
> *Mankind must different burdens know:*
> *Each bear his own, th'Apostle spoke:*
> *And chiefly they who bear the yoke.*
> *From wise subordination's plan*
> *Springs the chief happiness of man.* (lines 181-8)

Boswell was no poet, and it will be clear from these quotations that the bulk of *No Abolition of Slavery* is worthy of inclusion in any anthology of bad verse. Yet when he makes the only telling point in his argument – that the British working class and the demoralised *lumpenproletariat* of London live in conditions far worse than those of plantation slaves – the verse *does* achieve a certain quality reminiscent (though at a lower level) of Swift's poems of the city, or even of Blake's attitude to the "charter'd streets":

> *Look round this land of freedom, pray,*
> *And all its lower ranks survey:*
> *Bid the hard-working labourer speak,*
> *What are his scanty gains a week?*
> *All huddled in a smoaky shed,*
> *How are his wife and children fed?*
> *Are not the poor in constant fear*
> *Of the relentless Overseer?*
>
> *LONDON! Metropolis of bliss!*
> *Ev'n there sad sights we cannot miss:*
> *Beggars at every corner stand*
> *With doleful look and trembling hand:*
> *Here the shrill piteous cry of* sweep,
> *See wretches riddling an ash heap:*
> *The streets some for old iron scrape,*
> *And scarce the crush of wheels escape:*
> *Some share with dogs the half-eat bones,*
> *From dunghills pick'd with weary groans.*   (lines 191-207)

Boswell sets against slumland an idealised picture of the "cheerful gang" of slaves singing at their "task of industry . . . while time flies quick on downy wing" (lines 244-6). On the plantations, they even have the equivalents of sickness benefit and retirement pensions!

> *Finish'd the bus'ness of the day,*
> *No human beings are more gay:*
> *Of food, clothes, cleanly lodging sure,*
> *Each has his property secure:*
> *Their wives and children are protected,*
> *In sickness they are not neglected:*
> *And when old age brings a release,*
> *Their grateful days they end in peace.*   (lines 247-54)

Boswell makes the leap to conventional love-poetry through the age-old conceit that the lover is the slave of his mistress. In a grotesque analogy he depicts himself as a "fierce black" (because of his own dark complexion) who is transported "between the decks of hope and fear" by his "beauteous tyrant" to "Paphos isle" (Cyprus, the island of Aphrodite, where the goddess is supposed to have landed when she emerged from the sea). The poem then moves forward to its crowning ideological conceit — a peculiar application of Pope's argument in the

Essay on Man that the Great Chain of Being and the Chain of Love that binds the natural world are one and the same — that to abolish slavery "would be in vain/Since love's strong empire must remain". The poem ends bathetically:

> For Slavery there must ever be,
> While we have Mistresses like Thee!

As 1791 wore on, the news from France seemed more and more alarming to conservatives. It seems certain that Boswell would have agreed with Temple's hurried comment in a letter of July 1791, after the King's flight to Varennes on 20/21 June and his ignominious return to Paris four days later: "Alas! the poor king and queen of France, who could have imagined their subjects such Barbarians! O the noble-minded Burke! how I love him for his defence of injured, insulted Majesty and Nobility." (MS Yale C 2912). At about the same time, Boswell in London was becoming increasingly concerned at the impending celebration of the French Revolution by English supporters at the Crown and Anchor Tavern on 14 July. He did his best to dissuade his friend the Reverend Andrew Kippis, the scholarly editor of the second edition of the *Biographica Britannica*. from attending, writing to him on 11 July:

> I earnestly renew my request to you not to give the sanction of your presence to the meeting which is to be held on the 14th current to celebrate the anniversary of the French Revolution. My relation & friend Bosville has made my mind easy on his account by withdrawing himself to the continent so that he will not act as one of the Stewards. I mean not to throw out any reflections against those gentlemen who think it fit to assist at such a celebration in our Metropolis; but feeling so strongly upon the subject in a way different from what I am to suppose they do, I am truly anxious that they with whom I am more closely connected than by the social ties common to all fellow citizens, should not be partakers in the business.
>
> No man is a warmer and more determined foe to despotism and oppression than I am or could more sincerely rejoice at a rational and temperate reformation of the abuses of the french government, a reformation of which I with great pleasure observed the progress in a constitutional meeting of the states

of that Kingdom under their monarch as a free agent. But when seditious and unprincipled spirits violently overturned that constitutional system, destroyed all limits, trampled upon all establishments, let loose the wild fury of a Multitude amounting to twenty four millions and in short produced all the horrours of a barbarous anarchy, it appeared to me that the change was infinitely for the worse, and I shuddered to think of its immediate effects in France and nonbenevolence towards the nations around. . . .

In that hot fever are the french at this moment. Though there are some symptoms of abatement the crisis is not yet come. May GOD grant a favourable turn. You and I differ widely in our notions of policy both ecclesiastical and civil, but we differ as friends and men of candour who make mutual allowance. Oblige me then dear Dr Kippis by abstaining from celebrating the Anniversary of the French Revolution at least till it is certain that it is a Revolution upon the whole beneficial to Mankind. (MS Yale L 830)

Kippis replied immediately, saying that he *would* go to the celebration, and that he could not see how his "exultation" at what the French had achieved was incompatible with his "firmest attachment to the British Constitution, and the illustrious House of Hanover" (From Kippis, 12 July 1791, MS Yale C 1665). Boswell, for his part, had wrought himself into such a frenzy of disapproval that he sent several paragraphs to the newspapers ridiculing the forthcoming event, and on the great day itself, six satirical pieces in *The Times* entitled *Songs, parodies and choruses for the Celebration of the Glorious Revolution in France: By which Twenty-five Millions of civilized People are reduced from a great and ancient Monarchical Government to a Savage Anarchy.* The songs were assigned to various statesmen and publicists, most of whom are now forgotten. They are "in character", as if Boswell had imagined some ballad-opera in which they all took part, and they are set to tunes too familiar to contemporaries to be named. The best known person satirised was Joseph Priestley, whose house near Birmingham was wrecked by the mob on the evening of this very fourteenth of July, and nearly all his books, papers and scientific apparatus destroyed. Boswell's song of eleven short lines manages to bring in his researches into air and electricity, his unitarianism, and his belief in the psycho-physical unity of man which led to his being considered an atheist:

> *Socinian hymns prepare, Sir,*
> *Nought shall be FIX'D but AIR, Sir:*
>   *With electric shock,*
>   *Church and State let's knock,*
> *O! their downfall will be rare, Sir!*
>   *Drink about,*
>   *See it out,*
> *In MATTER only joy we find:*
>   *When man dies,*
>   *There he lies,*
> *Trust me Boys there is no MIND.*

The only song parodied that is at all familiar today, *The Little Ploughboy* ("A flaxen-headed cowboy"), provides the signature tune for a popular BBC radio programme for farmers. Boswell uses it to satirise a Scots immigrant who helped to finance the proceedings:

> *WILLIAM CUNNINGHAM, ESQ.*
> *A flaxen-headed Scottish boy*
>   *As simple as may be,*
> *Will do his best to share the joy*
>   *At France's anarchy.*
>
> *As STEWARD now promoted,*
>   *To help to pay the bill,*
> *His pockets he will empty fast,*
>   *His head with stuff to fill.*
>
> *When on the table dancing wild,*
>   *So great a man he'll be,*
> *You'll forget the simple Scottish boy:*
>   *Or scarcely know 'tis he.*

After it was all over, he wrote to Burke on 16 July:

> That Meeting I understand lost all its vivifying principle of Mischief, which was chilled by fear. They who ventured to attend were with very few exceptions men of little Consequence; and under the Cloak of decency they slunk away at an early hour like pusillanimous conspirators who were very glad to get out of such a scrape.[27]

Boswell was quite wrong here. At least nine hundred people attended, and the dinner went off very decorously.[28]

The year 1792 saw the spread in London and all over Britain of reform associations of various types – the Constitutional Society (an older, moribund body now revived), the Whig "Society of Friends of the People", the Corresponding Societies, and in Scotland political associations were formed not just in Edinburgh and Glasgow but in Dundee, Perth, Paisley, Kirkintilloch, Dalkeith, Montrose, Kilmarnock, Stirling, and Fife.[29] The growth of the reform movement does not seem to have been at all impeded by the news of the imprisonment of the French royal family in the Temple in August and the September massacres of imprisoned aristocrats. Thus towards the end of the year a delegate meeting of the Associated Friends of the People in Edinburgh summoned a convention of representatives of Scottish reform societies to meet there early in December. As the news from France deteriorated, it was only natural that the Right should hit back by forming their own associations, and that the clubbable Boswell should be drawn towards them. He joined no less than two. The first was private and élitist; its leading light was William Windham, whom Boswell had already featured in *No Abolition of Slavery*. After a dinner party at his home on 4 November 1792, Windham asked Boswell and French Laurence (Regius Professor of Civil Law at Oxford and Burke's literary executor) to stay behind:

> Windham, Laurence, and I remained some time by ourselves, and talked with earnestness of the seditious exertions in Britain, founded on a wild approbation of the proceedings in France. We agreed in thinking that it was the duty of our Government to take speedy and vigorous measures to check such sedition and not suffer it to increase and strengthen, and Windham thought that men of this way of thinking should meet prudently and concert what ought to be done. Laurence and I agreed in this. I felt as if in the reign of Charles I. (Journal)

Six weeks later the club was formed:

> Dined at Sir William Scott's with Lord Radnor, Mr Burke and his son, Dr Laurence, Mr Malone, Mr Metcalfe, Mr Cholmondeley, Sir Charles Bunbury, and Mr Windham, all *good men and true* for our excellent Constitution. Mr Burke proposed as a toast, "Old England against New France", and it having been proposed that we should be a club, Burke

asked us for next Sunday; but Windham having insisted on its being at his house on that day, it was so settled. (Journal, 16 December 1792)

The other revolutionary society which Boswell joined was a more public one, the Crown and Anchor Association which got its name from the tavern where it met and where, ironically enough, the reformist Constitutional Society held its gatherings in the room below. Its founder, John Reeves, had been a lawyer in Canada.[30] Boswell met him on 26 December, along with the treasurer, John Topham, barrister and antiquarian, who had been librarian to the Archbishop of Canterbury (Journal). Although it is not known when Boswell joined the Crown and Anchor group (its full title was "Association for Preserving Liberty and Property against Republicans and Levellers"), he claimed three months later to have been "one of the earliest Associators at the Crown and Anchor" (To Andrew Erskine, 6 March 1793). At its inaugural meeting on 20 November the Association produced a statement of principle headed "Considerations and Resolutions", which we must assume Boswell adhered to. The manifesto begins by stating that the Association's aim is to oppose erroneous opinions and the clubs and societies that promote them:

> These opinions are conveyed in the terms — *The Rights of Man* — *Liberty and Equality* — *No King* — *No Parliament* — and others of like import; all of them, in the sense imposed on them, expressing sentiments in direct opposition to the Laws of this Land, and some of them such as are inconsistent with the well-being of Society under any laws whatsoever.

The most pernicious of the Rights of Man is Equality, which, if realised in Britain, would utterly destroy our wellbeing and prosperity. The statement roundly assails the revolutionaries of France:

> It is with grief we see that in a neighbouring country the carrying into practice of this wild doctrine of *Equality* and the *Rights of Man,* has already produced these evils, and others ten thousand times greater. It is not yet publicly known, nor can it enter into the gentle heart of a BRITON to conceive, the number of atrocious crimes against God and man, that have been committed in support of these opinions. Murders and assassinations have been deliberately planned, and justified by some of these pretended philosophers, as the means to

attain their ends of reform. With all their pretences and promises, they have proceeded to violate every right, Civil and Natural, that should have been observed towards their Equals; — the people, who have only changed their masters, groan under new tyrannies of which they never heard or dreamed; and are subjected to the chastisement of one desperate leader after another. The excesses of these ruffian Demagogues have no bounds: they have already surpassed the wildest phrenzies of Fanaticism, Superstition, and Enthusiasm; plundering and murdering at home, and propagating their opinions by the sword in foreign countries; imposture, fallacy, falsehood, and bloodshed; their philosophy is the idle talk of schoolboys; and their actions are the savage ferociousness of wild beasts.

Britons, in fact, have all the Rights of Man they need:

It is well known, and we feel it daily, that we have as much of these pretended new inventions, as is necessary and convenient for a well-ordered Society. Every one has all the *Rights of Man* that leave him at liberty to do good to himself and his neighbour, and (what is worth considering) to protect his person and property against open or secret plunderers. He has as much of *Equality* as one man can possess without diminishing the Equality of his neighbour. We are told by our Religion (for *We* have a Religion, that we are *to do unto all men as we would that men should do unto us*); and this is realized to us by the firm administration of the Law; which suffers no injury to go without a remedy, and affords a remedy equally to the proudest and the poorest.

The manifesto ends by proposing five practical aims, the three most important being to suppress seditious publications and support "a due execution of the Laws made for the protection of persons and property"; to convince the public that the measures being canvassed by "perverted men" were not applicable to Britain; and to promote similar societies throughout the country.

In this same month of December, Boswell was being told by Temple that disaffection and sedition were rife in rural Cornwall;

It is amazing how that scoundrel Pains Rights are circulating here & what harm they do even among the lowest of the people; their very children have got the *cant*. They certainly talk very wildly. (1 December 1792, MS Yale C 2929)

He went into more detail ten days later, in an account of the polarisation of class attitudes and opinions which could have been parallelled from many other parts of the British Isles, not least Scotland, and which documents how speedily the propaganda of the Crown and Anchor Association was being disseminated in the provinces:

> The lowest of the People talk strangely here; but every body that has any thing dreads a Change & is firmly attached to the present Government. Mrs T. went this afternoon to pay a trifle to an old woman who keeps a little shop – Well, madam, I will take it as long as they will let me. I have lived too long to see such times, & will pray for the king with my last breath, God bless me – The children say to Octavius [Temple's schoolboy son] in Penryn, a civil war will be better for us poor folks, we shall get something. The maid at Laura's school says, my poor *fether* perhaps will get £20 or £30 a year, even Tucker, my labourer whom you recollect says to the servants in the kitchen, my wages at least will be raised & I shall live better. . . . Great pains have been taken to circulate Pains Pamphlet which has done more harm than you can conceive among the rabble . . . I hear to-day that Sir Francis Basset called The Tinners [tin-miners] together (a numerous body of men) & harangued them on the subject to very good effect: there is no fear of their Loyalty. He has also dispersed many hundred copies of the Paper from the association at the Crown and Anchor. I have reason to believe that association will be entered into here in every town & part of the County. I have also caught the contagion of Loyalty & the end of this week shall send my circular printed letter to the Clergy of two hundred & fifteen parishes or Churches. The original view was to recommend the County Library, but I zealously seize the opportunity to thunder against the madness & the wickedness of the French, to reprobate all Innovation whatever, at such a crisis as this & to affirm what I believe, our own present Government to be the wisest & the best that mankind in any age or any Country of the world, were ever blessed with; & I trust it will occasion a *Sensation* (as the French used to say) & do some good. (From Temple, 11 December, 1792, MS Yale C 2930)

Contemporary newspapers would apprise Boswell of the details of the King's execution on 21 January 1793 in terms similar to the report in *The Gentleman's Magazine* for that month:

> The Place de Louis Quinze, now called the Place of the Revolution, was the spot appointed for the MURDER. The place was filled with prodigious multitudes of people, and large bodies of horse and foot were drawn up to protect the execution. The most awful silence prevailed, while the coach was advancing slowly to the scaffold. The dying Monarch ascended it with heroic fortitude, with a firm step, and undismayed countenance. He was accompanied on the scaffold by his Confessor, and two or three Municipal Officers. In the middle stood the block, and near it two large ill-looking brutes, one of whom held the axe in his hand. The King for a moment looked around upon the people, with eyes which beamed forgiveness and love; and he was preparing himself to address the spectators, when, horrid to relate! one of the officers cried out "No Speeches; − come, no Speeches"; and suddenly the drums beat, and the trumpets sounded. He spoke, but all the expressions that could be distinctly heard were these: "I forgive my enemies: may God forgive them; and not lay my innocent blood to the charge of the Nation: God bless my People!!!" (Vol. 63 pp. 85-6)

Boswell responded by conceiving a scheme to erect a monument to the French King in Westminster Abbey. He drafted an eloquent call for subscriptions on 31 January:

> Monument in Honour of Louis XVI, King of France
> The anarchy, assassination, and sacrilege by which the King-dom of France has been disgraced, desolated, and polluted for some years past cannot but have excited the strongest emotions of horror in every virtuous Briton. But within these days our hearts have been pierced by the recital of proceedings in that country more brutal than any recorded in the annals of the world. Not contented with murdering their sovereign with every circumstance of rude and barbarous insult, previous to and during the execrable act the ruffians who have now usurped the power of France not only inhumanly refused to allow his remains to be reposited in the sepulchre of his

> fathers but with unexampled malignity have taken measures
> to prevent that honour being paid to him at any future time.
> To express therefore to surrounding nations and to posterity
> the generous indignation and abhorrence felt by the humane,
> free, and happy subjects of this realm at such savage atrocity,
> it is proposed that a subscription be opened for a monument
> to be erected in Westminster Abbey, the venerable repository
> of our own monarchs, to the memory of Louis XVI, King of
> France, whose patience, piety, dignified deportment, and
> fortitude in his last moments entitle him to the admiration of
> mankind.[31]

The appeal was never published, because the government dis-
approved of the scheme. Boswell's last public pronouncement on the
Revolution occurs in his "Advertisement to the Second Edition of the
Life of Johnson", 1 July 1793, where he claims that a reading of the *Life*
would "prove an effectual antidote to that detestable sophistry which
has been lately imported from France, under the false name of *Philosophy*, and with a malignant industry has been employed against the
peace, good order, and happiness of society, in our free and prosperous
country". More important by far was a purely personal involvement in
the following month. France had declared war on England and Holland
ten days after the King's execution, and by the summer British troops
were fighting on the continent alongside Prussians and Austrians.
Now Boswell had always believed that the English Bosvilles, who had
estates in Yorkshire, were the older and therefore superior branch of
his family, and he was particularly fond of Thomas Bosville, a colonel
with the British contingent of the Combined Armies in Flanders. His
death on 18 August was thus reported in *The Gentleman's Magazine* for
that month:

> Unfortunately killed in the action at the post of Lincelles,
> Lieut. Col. Bosville . . . [He] married but a short time
> before his departure with the guards, a lady of the name of
> Wilson, whom he has left pregnant. . . . He commanded
> the grenadier company of the second regiment; and was one
> of the tallest officers in the three regiments of guards, being
> six feet four inches high. He was shot through the mouth, the
> bullet having passed over the head of the Hon. Capt. Fitzroy,
> who was standing within a foot of him. (Vol. 63, ii, 774)

Boswell has left a vivid report of his reaction to the event:

> At breakfast I read in the newspaper that there had been an
> action in Flanders, in which Colonel Bosville was killed. This
> agitated me much, and I hastened to his friend Colonel
> Morrison of the Coldstream . . . I met a sergeant of the
> Coldstream, to whom I spoke, and was informed by him that
> the sad report was real. I found Colonel Morrison with tears
> in his eyes; he put into my hand a letter which he had just
> received from Captain Hewgill, adjutant to the Coldstream
> and secretary to the Duke of York, communicating the
> melancholy event. I was deeply affected − running back in
> my mind on the many scenes in which I had seen the Colonel
> since I first saw him a little boy at his father's in London. I
> called on Windham, who regretted him much; and he
> accompanied me first to the orderly room of the First Regi-
> ment of Guards, which I happened to know, and then to the
> office of Mr King, Under-Secretary of State, at both of which
> places we got more particulars. We afterwards walked to
> different places, and I parted with him in Long Acre and went
> to my brother at Somerset House, who joined me in condo-
> lence, saying that the Colonel was *an emblem of life*. It was
> indeed difficult for some time to bring our *imaginations* to
> *believe* that he was dead. We went together and left our cards
> at the lodgings of his brother, and then dined at my house. I
> was in a kind of distraction of mind from time to time. My
> *military ardour* was quite extinguished. I resolved not to go to
> the Continent this year. (Journal, 22 August)

The last two sentences refer to his plan (reminiscent of Pierre Bezuhov
in *War and Peace*) to visit the combat zone and view the action at first
hand. In the sardonic words of Marlies Danziger, "any notion of
personal glory, whether as great dramatist or wit or political adviser,
now gave way to the realization that the Revolution meant actual
danger and death − and not just for the French".[32]

In his journal entry for 24 December 1793 he set down what he
could remember of an interview he had with Lord Thurlow on some date
during May. When Thurlow had asked Boswell "what news there was":

> I said I heard of none except the accounts which we had from
> the Allied Army. Battles being mentioned, he said he had read

the history of *many*, but never could understand *one*. He had been lately reading the account of the battle of Minden, and it appeared to him that Prince Ferdinand must have been drunk, and that Lord George Sackville was the only man who knew anything about the matter. *Being now out of Administration,* he seemed to be adverse to the war against the French; yet when I asked him if he thought the old government of France oppressive, as now so loudly asserted, he exclaimed in his *swearing manner,* "Damn their bloods; there was not as much oppression under the old government as would justify shedding the blood of a single chimney-sweep".

And that is about the sum total of Boswell's remarks on the French Revolution, public or private. All the while, Temple was becoming more and more extreme in his detestation of what was happening across the Channel, at times appearing almost unbalanced. It seems reasonable to assume that Boswell's opinions followed a similar course.

On 30 January 1794, the anniversary of the execution of Charles I, he wrote to Boswell:

> I am just going to deprecate the vengeance of the Almighty from the Posterity of the actors of the horrid deed of this day, & which ourselves have seen repeated with aggravated circumstances of savage manners in a Country whose inhabitors ought to be wiped from the face of the Earth. Surely some dreadful calamity awaits them: indeed it is already begun & now rages with no small degree of fury. (MS Yale C 2954)

By 26 May the revolutionaries were "enemies of whatever is sacred and valuable in human life" (MS Yale C 2969), and on 3 June he made a shrewd comment on the inconsistency of his democrat neighbour, the landlord Richard Lovell Gwatkin of Killion: "with all his prejudice for the Sans Culottes, no one is more vigorous in putting the game laws in force & harassing an unqualified person for killing a hare or a partridge". (MS Yale C 2972). In one of his many letters to Temple which have not survived, Boswell reported that he had been reading Clarendon's *History of the Rebellion.* In view of what we know of his feelings towards the Stuarts, there can be no doubt that he must have agreed wholeheartedly with his friend's parallel between seventeenth-century fanaticism and "modern" revolutionary excesses:

> The *cant* of those times is unaccountable; one cannot reconcile

their actions & practices with the strain of their speeches, professions &c. It seems that at periods the publick mind is subject to a species of Delirium. Such was the case here during Clarendons times, & one has some reason to dread that something of the same kind will happen next all over Europe. How opinions change! In early youth I rejoiced at the Fate of the unfortunate Charles. I now cannot read his sad story without tears & abhorrence of the fanatical & hypocritical miscreants who shed his sacred blood. If tyranny is unavoidable, let it be one of Gentlemen & not of the *Swinish* multitude: the expression, however exclaimed against by the factious & unexperienced shews Burkes thorough acquaintance with mankind. The *pious* & what some would call the *superstitious* turn of our noble historian is far more congenial with my sentiments than the Sceptical or Irreligious ones that pollute the pages of Modern *Dissertations* & wd deprive us of all trust & confidence in the Almighty. (From Temple, 15 January 1795, MS Yale C 2977)

Two months later, when there was a move in the Lords for peace negotiations, Temple wrote:

I hope the Nation in general do not wish for Peace. No city of consequence & no County has yet petitioned. Is it not provoking to hear noble Lords declaiming in such a strain in the Upper House? One wd. imagine they had lost their senses or were retained by our enemies. Lord S. should be sent to Bedlam; Lord L. confined to his house in Scotland, & the Marquess of L. transported to America, to console & assist his quondam Librarian in endeavouring to Republicanize all the Kingdoms of Europe. Surely a spirit of Delirium has seized the public mind. (5 March 1795, MS Yale C 2979)

After this, we have only two very brief letters from Temple to Boswell, and four dictated by Boswell during his last illness to his son, James the younger. By 19 May 1795 the Great Biographer was dead.

6. *Burns* 1789-1796

Although it is likely that Burns became a "votary of France" as early as 1789, we have no certain evidence of his feelings about the Revolution till the 1790s. The following may well be the earliest of Burns's writings to show awareness of what was happening in France:

> To the beautiful Miss Eliza J—n, on her principles of
> Liberty and Equality
> *How Liberty, girl, can it be by thee nam'd?*
> *Equality too! hussey, art not asham'd;*
> *Free and Equal indeed; while mankind thou*
> *enchainest,*
> *And over their hearts a proud Despot so reignest.*

The piece cannot be dated precisely and it is not even certain who Miss J—n was. Although James Kinsley placed it in 1788 it is tempting to assign it to mid or late 1789 at the earliest, because of its use of what were to become two of the three great revolutionary catchwords.

At the end of 1791 Burns moved with his family from the farm of Ellisland to three small rooms above the Stamp Office in the Wee Vennel (now Bank Street) in Dumfries: he was now a full-time excise officer, and soon allied himself with the radical elements in town. From autumn 1794 these included his physician, William Maxwell, who had studied medicine in France and actually served as a guard during the execution of Louis XVI and was the proud possessor of a handkerchief which had then been dipped in the King's blood.[33] Burns's most picturesque exploit as an exciseman was his part in the capture of the smuggling schooner *Rosamond* at the end of February 1792. Our principal authority is the journal of Riding Officer Walter Crawford. On the 26th he learned that a landing of smugglers was imminent, and on the 27th

> My Express arrived informing me that a landing was making or about to be made, on which I set off with Mr Lewars directly, leaving Messrs Burns, Penn & Ranking to follow as fast as possible.

The Excise summoned the military, and after various contretemps (the country people had staved in every boat on the coast to prevent the excise party using them to board the smuggler), on the 29th

> We drew up the Millitary in three divisions determined to approach her & attact her if the s[t]ream was foardable, one

party fore and aft and the Third on her Broadside, the first party being Commanded by Quarter Master Manly, the Second by my self and the Third led by Mr Burns.

Our orders to the Millitary were to reserve there fire till within eight yards of the vessel, then to pour a volley and board her with sword & Pistol. The vessel kept on firing thou[gh] without any damage to us, as from the situation of the ship they could not bring their great guns to bear on us, we in the mean time wading breast high, and in Justice to the party under my Command I must say with great alacrity; by the time we were within one hundred yards of the vessel the Crew gave up the cause, gott over side towards England which shore was for a long way dry sand.

The National Library of Scotland has, in Burns's hand, a record of the guarding, repair and floating of the vessel and her preparation for sale. Burn's colleague in the excise, John Lewars, also kept a journal (since disappeared) recording that Burns bought four carronades (short cannon of large bore) at the sale for £3. These he sent to the revolutionary government in France — a perfectly legal proceeding, since Britain and France were still at peace — but they were apparently intercepted by the customs at Dover, though we have no documentary proof of the interception.[34]

Such a dramatic gesture was not calculated to impress Burns's superiors in the Excise, and there was more to follow. On 13 November 1792 he subscribed to the *Edinburgh Gazetteer* whose editor, Captain William Johnston, was soon to be imprisoned in the drive against sedition. And there were strange goings-on in the Dumfries theatre around that time, which are touched on in Burns's letter to Mrs Dunlop of 6 December:

We, in this country, here have many alarms of the Reform, or rather the Republican spirit, of your part of the kingdom. — Indeed, we are a good deal in commotion ourselves, & in our Theatre here, "God save the king" has met with some groans & hisses, while, Ça ira has been repeatedly called for. — For me, I am a *Placeman*, you know; a very humble one indeed, Heaven knows, but still so much so as to gag me from joining in the cry. — What my private sentiments are, you will find out without an Interpreter. — In the mean time, I have taken up the subject in another view, and the other day, for a pretty

Actress's benefit-night, I wrote an Address, which I will give on the other page, called "The Rights of Woman".

THE RIGHTS OF WOMAN
An Occasional Address
Spoken by Miss Fontenelle on her Benefit Night
November 26, 1792

While Europe's eye is fix'd on mighty things,
The fate of empires and the fall of kings;
While quacks of State must each produce his plan,
And even children lisp the Rights of Man;
Amid this mighty fuss just let me mention,
The Rights of Woman merit some attention.

First, in the sexes' intermix'd connexion
One sacred Right of Woman is Protection:
The tender flower, that lifts its head elate,
Helpless must fall before the blasts of fate,
Sunk on the earth, defac'd its lovely form,
Unless your shelter ward th'impending storm.

Our second Right — but needless here is caution —
To keep that right inviolate's the fashion:
Each man of sense has it so full before him,
He'd die before he'd wrong it — 'tis Decorum!
There was, indeed, in far less polish'd days,
A time, when rough rude Man had naughty ways:
Would swagger, swear, get drunk, kick up a riot,
Nay, even thus invade a lady's quiet!
Now, thank our stars! these Gothic times are fled;
Now, well-bred men — and you are all well-bred —
Most justly think (and we are much the gainers)
Such conduct neither spirit, wit, nor manners.

For Right the third, our last, our best, our dearest:
That right to fluttering female hearts the nearest,
Which even the Rights of Kings, in low prostration,
Most humbly own — 'tis dear, dear Admiration!
In that blest sphere alone we live and move;
There taste that life of life — Immortal Love.
Smiles, glances, sighs, tears, fits, flirtations, airs —
'Gainst such an host what flinty savage dares?

> *When awful Beauty joins with all her charms,*
> *Who is so rash as rise in rebel arms?*
> *But truce with kings, and truce with constitutions,*
> *With bloody armaments and revolutions;*
> *Let Majesty your first attention summon:*
> *Ah! ça ira! the Majesty of Woman!*

It is probable that most of Miss Fontenelle's audience knew of Paine's *Rights of Man* (1791-92), and Burns perhaps assumed that some would be aware of Mary Wollstonecraft's *Vindication of the Rights of Women*, published earlier in the year. Burns's "Rights of Women" are not those of social equality, however, but such as befit "the weaker sex" and are graciously vouschafed by the superior male. Yet there is an irony in the paragraph on decorum which is lost on the modern reader but would seem charged with class feeling to the original hearers. All would be uncomfortably aware that precious few of Miss Fontenelle's audience were in fact well bred, and that woman's second right — "Decorum" — was continually flouted by the local gentry in boorish exhibitions of drunken hooliganism, as can be deduced from a letter from John Syme, Distributor of Stamps in Dumfries and a warm friend of Burns, about the Caledonian Hunt's visit to Dumfries two years later:

> Our Caledonian Hunt went off with dissipation without fashionable gaiety — There was not one of Noble blood at the Races if we except Maule — the exhibitions of the Bucks were splendid if we give that title to rioting. Drinking three bottles each day, disturbing the players, staggering in at the Assembly — some even dancing in boots — displayed the spirit and genius of modern manners — Baker, one of the knowing english Squires on the Turf made an elegant appearance by insulting in the grossest manner Squire Walter Riddel of this place who pursued him to Durham and made him ask pardon which is published in our papers of last week. Maule and others you would hear, pickled our friend Harry Welsh — by daubing his hair with mustard etc & sticking toothpic quills in it by way of hedgehogging the man — This lad, Cunningham, must be distracted — his behaviour here has been horrible and I dare say will make a desert about him if ever he appears again in this quarter. (Syme to Alexander Cunningham, 21 November 1794)[35]

It will be remembered from the last section that November 1792 was precisely the month when the Crown and Anchor Association was founded in England and the anti-revolutionary forces were beginning their counter-attack on the radicals. Scotland followed suit only nine days later, with the setting up of the Goldsmith's Hall Association in Edinburgh "to counteract all seditious attempts, and in particular, all associations for the publication or dispersion of seditious and inflammatory writings, or tending to excite disorders and tumults within this part of the kingdom".[36] It is therefore not surprising that Burns was in serious trouble only a month after the hissing of "God Save the King" and the calls for "Ça ira". His superior, Collector Mitchell, told him he had been ordered by the Excise Board to inquire into his "political conduct", and accused him of being "a person disaffected to Government". On 31 December Burns wrote off to Robert Graham of Fintry, Commissioner of the Scottish Board of Excise, in great alarm at the prospect of seeing "the much-loved wife of [my] bosom, & [my] helpless prattling little ones, turned adrift into the world, degraded & disgraced from a situation in which they had been respectable & respected, & left almost without the necessary support of a miserable existence". He protested his innocence and his adherence to the principles of the Glorious [British] Revolution of 1688:

> I believe, Sir, I may aver it, & in the sight of Omnipotence, that I would not tell a deliberate Falsehood, no, not though even worse horrors, if worse can be, than those I have mentioned, hung over my head; & I say, that the allegation, whatever villain has made it, is a *Lie!* To the British Constitution, on Revolution principles, next after my God, I am most devoutly attached!

But he seems to have given a somewhat different account to Mrs Dunlop. On the very same day of his letter to Graham he told her that "some envious, malicious devil has raised a little demur on my political principles . . . I have set, henceforth a seal on my lips, as to these unlucky politics; but to you, I must breathe my sentiments". Unfortunately, the page and a half outlining these sentiments has been torn away, apart from the following fragments, from which we can deduce their tenor:

> War I deprecate: misery & ruin to thousands, are in the blast that announces the destructive Demon. – But . . . [missing

section} . . . the wisdom of their wickedness, & wither the
strength of their iniquity! Set this seal upon their unrighteous
resolves, "Behold, whatsoever you do, it shall not prosper.
That destruction THOU hast already begun to deal unto
them, may it be the for . . ." [missing section]

The "they" and "their" of this mangled effusion cannot refer to those
who had put the King on trial five days before, when one considers the
time taken to get express mail from Paris to London, and then to print
and distribute newspapers with an all-British circulation in those
days. And if they referred to the revolutionary armies which had
conquered Belgium and were now threatening Holland, his fulmina-
tion can only have been a temporary outburst tailored for the occasion,
for it was as recently as 12 December that he had poked fun at France's
enemies in "When Princes and Prelates and het-headed zealots":

> When Brunswick's great Prince cam a cruising to France
>   Republican billies to cowe,
> Bauld Brunswick's great Prince wad hae shawn better sense,
>   At hame with his Princess to mowe. —   fuck
>   And why should na poor folk mowe, &c.
>
> Out over the Rhine proud Prussia wad shine,
>   To spend his best blood he did vow:
> But Frederic had better ne'er forded the water,
>   But spent as he docht in a mowe. — (Stanzas 2, 3)   had the power

The fifth stanza is evidence of how well-informed Burns was about
European events such as the second partition of Poland:

> Auld Kate laid her claws on poor Stanislaus,
>   And Poland has bent like a bow:
> May the deil in her arse ram a huge prick o' brass!
>   And damn her in Hell with a mowe!
>   And why &c.

On 18 May 1792 Russia declared war on Poland and marched to the
gates of Warsaw: on 23 July Stanlislaus of Poland (who had once been
Catharine II's lover) submitted to the Empress, an armistice was
concluded and the command of the Polish army was consigned to a
Russian general. But it was not till July 1793 that the second partition
of Poland was completed, long after Burns's song was written.

Burns evidently felt that "When Princes and Prelates" was not an
incendiary document, for he enclosed it in a letter to Graham of Fintry

on 5 January with the clear implication that the song was politically innocuous. In that letter he replied one by one to the charges that had been laid against him: namely, that he had been the leader of those who had hissed "God save the King" and called for "Ça ira"; that he had uttered invectives against the King; that he had advocated extreme "reform principles"; that he was in correspondence with Captain Johnston of the radical *Gazetteer:* and that he was an extreme partisan of France. Burns answered the last accusation in these terms:

> As to France, I was her enthusiastic votary in the beginning of the business. — When she came to shew her old avidity for conquest, in annexing Savoy &c. to her dominions, & invading the rights of Holland, I altered my sentiments.

When Graham of Fintry conveyed Burns's answers to the Board, the last "gave great offence", and William Corbet, General Supervisor of Excise, was ordered to go down to Dumfries and personally interrogate the poet, "& to document me — 'that *my* business was to *act*, not to think; & that whatever might be Men or Measures, it was for me to be silent and obedient'" (To John Francis Erskine of Mar, 13 April 1793). Corbet's visitation seems to have taken place in January and to have been a highly civilised proceeding, according to John Syme — "Mr Corbet admonished Burns — but found no grounds, save some witty sayings — Mr Corbet, Mr Finlater [Supervisor of Excise, Dumfries] Burns & I dined together once or twice on the occasion".[37] On 1 February France declared war on England and Holland and the government seriously began to silence the democratic associations in the country. Yet despite all his protestations to Fintry about France's "old avidity for conquest", Burns continued to express pro-French opinions and write pro-French songs, though not to publish them.

After Dumouriez, the general who had gained brilliant victories for France in 1792, went over to the Austrians on 4 April, Burns wrote a scornful "Address" to him which begins "You're welcome to Despots, Dumourier" and ends (the persona is presumably the Austrian Emperor):

> *Then let us fight about, Dumourier:*
> *Then let us fight about, Dumourier:*
> *Then let us fight about,*
> *'Till freedom's spark is out,*
> *Then we'll be damned no doubt — Dumourier.*

In midsummer, the war news and his historical reading made him

"burst with indignation" at "these mighty villains who divide kingdom against kingdom, desolate provinces & lay Nations waste out of
the wantonness of Ambition", as he wrote to his musical publisher
George Thomson at the end of June, enclosing a song about a woman
separated by war from her husband:

> O wae upon you, Men o' State,
> That brethren rouse in deadly hate!
> As ye make monie a fond heart mourn,
> Sae may it on your heads return!
> Ye mindna 'mid your cruel joys
> The widow's tears, the orphan's cries:
> But soon may peace bring happy days,
> And Willie hame to Logan braes!
>
> ("O Logan, sweetly didst thou glide", lines 25-32)

At the end of August he sent Thomson "Scots Wha Hae", to the
tune "Hey tuttie taitie", which tradition held was Robert Bruce's
march to Bannockburn. The air, he told Thomson, produced "accidental recollection of that glorious struggle for Freedom [the Scottish
War of Independence]", and became "associated with the glowing
ideas of some other struggles of the same nature, *not quite so ancient*":
the finest of all Scottish patriotic songs was the result. The earliest of
these recent struggles were no doubt the Fifteen and the Forty-five,
but the song's militant forward thrust, its use of "tyrants" as a code
word for "despots" (the Revolution's term for the kings of contemporary Europe), and the new associations which had in recent years
clustered around the word "liberty", indicate that the main parallels
were with France and the British reformers. Writing to Mrs Dunlop
some three months later, Burns presents his song as entirely a work of
the historical imagination: "One favored hour of my Muse, I was
reading the history of the battle of Bannockburn, & figuring to myself
the looks & feelings of the Scots Patriot Heroes on that eventful day, as
they saw their hated but powerful Tyrants advance", and he here gives
it the title of "Bruce's Speech to his troops" (15 December, 1793).
Certainly the last stanza ("Tyrants fall in every foe") contains a superb
transformation of the account of the battle of Biggar in Blind Harry's
Wallace, as rendered in Hamilton of Gilbertfield's eighteenth-century
version:

> Here pride, ambition, arms each guilty foe,
> And tyranny attends on every blow.

Nevertheless, it seems clear that the song's revolutionary reverbera-
tions were uppermost in Burns's mind. That is the implication of his
cautious instruction to the editor of the reforming *Morning Chronicle,*
which published it on 8 May 1794: "they are most welcome to my
Ode; only, let them insert it as a thing they have met with by accident,
& unknown to me" (To Patrick Miller, Junior, mid-March 1794).

An opposition club to the Dumfries reformers, calling themselves
the "Loyal Natives", was established on 18 January 1793 for "Preserving Peace, Liberty, and Property" and for supporting "the Laws
and Constitution of the Country" — exactly the aims of the Crown
and Anchor Association which Boswell had joined in London. When
Burns read a "vehemently loyal" advertisement of theirs, he "spouted"
the following extempore (the word is Syme's):

> *Pray who are these* Natives *the rabble so ven'rate?*
> *They're our true ancient natives, and the breed unregen'rate:*
> *The ignorant savage that weather'd the storm,*
> *When the Man and the Brute differed but in the form.*[38]

At some point near the middle of 1794 one of these loyalists produced
the following squib, mentioning the leading democrats of the town:

> *Ye sons of sedition give ear to my song,*
> *Let Syme, Burns, and Maxwell pervade every throng,*
> *With Craken the attorney, and Mundell the quack,*
> *Send Willie the monger to hell with a smack.*

When it was handed to Burns he uttered these lines, again extempore:

> *Ye true "Loyal Natives", attend to my song,*
> *In uproar and riot rejoice the night long;*
> *From* envy *and* hatred *your corps is exempt;*
> *But where is your shield from the* darts of contempt?[39]

It seems probable that the rivalry between the Loyal Natives and the
Burns-Syme-Maxwell group had something to do with Burns's famous
ambiguous toast, "May our success in the present war be equal to the
justice of our cause", which almost got him into a duel with a Captain
Dods, in whose presence the toast was presumably made (To Samuel
Clarke Junior, June/July 1794). Tradition ascribes other and more
explicit toasts to Burns at this time, such as "To the last verse of the
last chapter of the last book of Kings".

A much more substantial piece than any of these quatrains, the "Ode for General Washington's Birthday", also dates from 1794. It was perhaps begun early in the year (Washington was born on 22 February) then laid aside till summer, for on 25 June Burns sent a draft of the last stanza to Mrs Dunlop, which "I have been framing as I passed along the road. The subject is, LIBERTY: you know . . . how dear the theme is to me". A considerable time before, perhaps in the early months of the Revolution, Burns had naturalised Liberty as a temperamental Highland filly in a delightful comic fragment "On Glenriddel's Fox breaking her chain", but now, three or four years later, she is a rhetorical personification, not a concretely realised metaphor. In the first stanza of the Ode the singer hymns her by taking Columbia's harp (the freedom kindled by the American colonists) to sing of the "broken chain" of imperial oppression and "dash it in a tyrant's face" (George III's). In the second stanza the theme is the "Wha wad fill a coward's grave/Wha sae base as be a slave" of "Scots wha hae":

> Avaunt! thou caitiff, servile, base,
> That tremblest at a despot's nod,
> Yet, crouching under th'iron rod,
> Canst laud the arm that struck th'insulting blow!
> Art thou of man's imperial line?
> Dost boast that countenance divine?
> Each skulking feature answers, No!
> But come, ye sons of Liberty,
> Columbia's offspring, brave as free,
> In danger's hour still flaming in the van:
> Ye know, and dare maintain, the Royalty of Man.   (lines 18-28)

In the third stanza, the subject is England. King Alfred, and all those English bards who throughout the ages have "rous'd the freeborn Briton's soul of fire" are adjured to desert her in the present age when she is waging a reactionary war against the champions of liberty:

> Dare injured nations form the great design,
> To make detested tyrants bleed?
> Thy England execrates the glorious deed!
> Beneath her hostile banners waving,
> Every pang of honour braving,
> England in thunders calls − "The Tyrant's cause is mine!"

> *That hour accurst, how did the fiends rejoice,*
> *And Hell thro' all her confines raise th'exulting voice!*
> *That hour which saw the generous English name*
> *Link't with such damned deeds of everlasting shame!*
>
> (lines 34-43)

The last stanza makes Scotland out to be as blamable as England, though for cowardice and debility rather than active, malevolent tyranny:

> *Thee, Caledonia, thy wild heaths among,*
> *Famed for the martial deed, the heaven-taught song,*
> *To thee I turn with swimming eyes!*
> *Where is that soul of Freedom fled?*
> *Immingled with the mighty Dead.*
> *Beneath that hallowed turf where Wallace lies!*
> *Hear it not, Wallace, in thy bed of death!*
> *Ye babbling winds, in silence sweep!*
> *Disturb not ye the hero's sleep,*
> *Nor give the coward secret breath!*
> *Is this the ancient Caledonian form,*
> *Firm as her rock, resistless as her storm?*
> *Shew me that eye which shot immortal hate,*
> *Blasting the Despot's proudest bearing!*
> *Shew me that arm which, nerved with thundering fate,*
> *Braved Usurpations's boldest daring!*
> *Dark-quenched as yonder sinking star,*
> *No more that glance lightens afar:*
> *That palsied arm no more whirls on the waste of war.*
>
> (lines 44-62)

In complete contrast, "A Man's a Man for a' that" is wholeheartedly positive throughout: so much so that one is tempted to date it from the earliest stage of Scottish radical support for the Revolution, when Paine's *Rights of Man* first swept the country. Yet we cannot with any certainty place it earlier than 1794, and near the end of the year at that, well after the most celebrated sedition trials. There exists a copy in Burns's hand in the Adam MS., once owned by R. B. Adam, New York, endorsed "Burns 1794": this would seem to place it near the end of December, when set beside the fact that Burns sent a copy to Thomson in a letter dated January 1795, prefixed by these ironically self-deprecating remarks: "A great critic, Aikin on songs, says, that love & wine are the exclusive themes for song-writing. The following is on neither subject, & consequently is no Song; but will be allowed, I think, to be two or three pretty good *prose* thoughts, inverted into rhyme." The prose was of course Tom Paine's, and not so much translated into rhyme as transformed into poetry, as can be easily seen when Burns's third and fourth stanzas are compared with relevant passages in Paine. Thus Burns (lines 9-16):

> *Ye see yon birkie ca'd a lord,*　　　　　conceited fellow
> 　*Wha struts, an' stares, an' a' that?*
> *Tho' hundreds worship at his word,*
> 　*He's but a cuif for a' that.*　　　　　　fool
> *For a' that, an' a' that,*
> 　*His ribband, star, an' a' that,*
> *The man o' independent mind,*
> 　*He looks an' laughs at a' that.*　　(lines 17-24)

And Paine:

> The French Constitution says, *There shall be no titles*; and, of consequence, all that class of equivocal generation which in some countries is called "aristocracy", and in others "nobility", is done away, and the *peer* is exalted into MAN . . . [Love of titles] talks about its fine *blue ribbon* like a girl, and shews its new *garter* like a child. (*Rights of Man*, Everyman Edn., p. 59)

Where Burns has:

> *A prince can mak a belted knight,*
> 　*A marquis, duke, an' a' that!*
> *But an honest man's aboon his might —*　　above
> 　*Guid faith, he mauna fa' that!*　must not lay claim to
> *For a' that, an' a' that,*
> 　*Their dignities, an' a' that,*
> *The pith o' sense an' pride o' worth*
> 　*Are higher rank than a' that,*　　(lines 25-32)

the original in Paine reads:

> The patriots of France have discovered in good time that rank and dignity in society must take a new ground. The old one

has fallen through. It must now take the substantial ground of character, instead of chimerical ground of titles. . . . The artificial NOBLE shrinks into a dwarf before the NOBLE of Nature . . . (pp. 60, 63).

Burns's last stanza ("Then let us pray . . .") is most closely paralleled by Paine's statement: "For what we can foresee, all Europe may form but one great Republic, and man be free of the whole" (p. 211). The concept of nationalism, earlier often present in a Jacobite form, has completely fused with that of freedom in "Scots Wha Hae"; now, in "A Man's a Man for a' That", it has been transcended in a blend of internationalism and the revolutionary ideal of Fraternity. As the French critic Auguste Angellier put it long ago, the song is "the *Marseillaise* of Equality", the anthem of the whole human race.[40]

In the very month in which he sent "A Man's a Man" to Thomson and two full years after he had assured Graham of Fintry he was no longer a "votary" of France, Burns was still able, in private, to condone and even praise the most violent actions of the revolutionaries. A tinge of plebeian vindictiveness colours the expression of his pro-French sympathies when writing to Mrs Dunlop. Four of her sons and one grandson were, or had been, in the army, and two of her daughters had married French refugees: her sympathies were naturally with the royalists, yet Burns did not hesitate to thrust his views upon her. His diatribe of 12 January 1795 was the last straw. A reading of Dr John Moore's *Journal during a Residence in France* (1793) prompted Burns to write:

> Entre nous, you know my Politics; & I cannot approve of the honest Doctor's whining over the deserved fate of a certain pair of Personages. — What is there in the delivering over a perjured Blockhead & an unprincipled Prostitute into the hands of the hangman, that it should arrest for a moment, attention, in an eventful hour, when, as my friend Roscoe in Liverpool gloriously expresses it —

> "When the welfare of Millions is hung in the scale
> And the balance yet trembles with fate!"[41]

Mrs Dunlop was apparently so offended that she stopped writing to him, though she relented shortly before Burns's death.

Burns's prose remarks about Louis XVI and Marie Antoinette may serve as prelude to one of the most intriguing poems in the whole Burns

canon — "The Tree of Liberty". We do not know for certain if Burns
was the author, nor when the poem was written. It was first published
by William and Robert Chambers in their edition of 1838, with the
note "here printed for the first time, from a MS. in the possession of
Mr James Duncan, Mosesfield, near Glasgow", but since then the
manuscript has never surfaced, and editors of Burns have felt free to
include or exclude it in accordance with their political prejudices.
Despite its length, it must be quoted in full:

> *Heard ye o' the tree o' France,*
> *I watna what's the name o't:*
> *Around it a' the patriots dance.*
> *Weel Europe kens the fame o't.*
> *It stands where ance the Bastile stood,*
> *A prison built by kings, man,*
> *When Superstition's hellish brood*
> *Kept France in leading strings, man.*

> *Upo' this tree there grows sic fruit,*   such
> *Its virtues a' can tell, man;*
> *It raises man aboon the brute,*   above
> *It maks him ken himsel, man*
> *Gif ance the peasant taste a bit,*
> *He's greater than a lord, man,*
> *An' wi' the beggar shares a mite*
> *O' a' he can afford, man.*

> *This fruit is worth a' Afric's wealth,*
> *To comfort us 'twas sent, man:*
> *To gie the sweetest blush o' health,*
> *An' mak us a' content, man.*
> *It clears the een, it cheers the heart,*   eyes
> *Maks high and low guid friends, man:*
> *And he wha acts the traitor's part*
> *It to perdition sends, man.*

> *My blessings aye attend the chiel*   fellow
> *Wha pitied Gallia's slaves, man,*
> *And staw a branch, spite o' the Deil,*   stole
> *Frae yont the western waves, man.*

Fair Virtue water'd it wi' care,
    And now she sees wi' pride, man,
How weel it buds and blossoms there,
    Its branches spreading wide, man.

But vicious folks aye hate to see
    The works o' Virtue thrive, man;
The courtly vermin's banned the tree,
    And grat to see it thrive, man;   *wept*
King Loui' thought to cut it down,
    When it was unco sma', man;   *very*
For this the watchman cracked his crown,
    Cut aff his head and a', man.

A wicked crew syne, on a time,   *then*
    Did tak a solemn aith, man,   *oath*
It ne'er should flourish to its prime,
    I wat they pledged their faith, man.   *know for certain*
Awa' they gaed wi' mock parade,   *went*
    Like beagles hunting game, man,
But soon grew weary o' the trade
    And wished they'd been at hame, man.

Fair Freedom, standing by the tree,
    Her sons did loudly ca', man;
She sang a sang o' liberty,
    Which pleased them ane and a', man.
By her inspired, the new-born race
    Soon drew the avenging steel, man;
The hirelings ran — her foes gied chase,   *gave*
    And banged the despot weel, man.

Let Britain boast her hardy oak,
    Her poplar and her pine, man,
Auld Britain ance could crack her joke,
    And o'er her neighbours shine, man.
But seek the forest round and round,
    And soon 'twill be agreed, man,
That sic a tree can not be found,
    Twixt London and the Tweed, man.

Without this tree, alake this life
  Is but a vale o' woe, man;
A scene o' sorrow mixed wi' strife,
  Nae real joys we know, man.
We labour soon, we labour late,
  To feed the titled knave, man;
And a' the comfort we're to get
  Is that ayont the grave, man.　　　　　　beyond

Wi' plenty o' sic trees, I trow,
  The warld would live in peace, man;
The sword would help to mak a plough,
  The din o' war wad cease, man.
Like brethren in a common cause,
  We'd on each other smile, man;
And equal rights and equal laws
  Wad gladden every isle, man.

Wae worth the loon wha wadna eat　woe befall the fellow
  Sic halesome dainty cheer, man;
I'd gie my shoon frae aff my feet,
  To taste sic fruit, I swear, man.
Syne let us pray, auld England may　　　　　Then
  Sure plant this far-famed tree, man;
And blythe we'll sing, and hail the day
  That gave us liberty, man.

In France, Trees of Liberty were a development of the trees country people used to plant in May to celebrate the arrival of Spring; apparently, the first of them was planted in a village in the Rhône valley in 1790. That is to say, the Tree of Liberty was a development of peasant culture and a gift of the countryside to the Revolution. The fashion spread like wildfire all over France, and it is estimated that "some 60,000 trees were planted in honour of Liberty in those days, all of them decorated with tricolor ribbons and red caps".[42] The fashion spread to Britain, and is much better documented for Scotland than for England: thus in November 1792 (about the time of Burns's troubles in the Dumfries theatre) the radicals of Perth set one up at the Cross in honour of General Dumouriez' entry into Brussels, while their brethren in Dundee erected one "decked with apples, a lantern, candles, and the slogan "LIBERTY, EQUALITY AND NO SINECURES".

After the suppression of the British Constitutional Convention of democratic reformers in Edinburgh at the end of 1793 and the arrest of its leaders on 5 December, the Tree was still a potent symbol; thus when one of them, Maurice Margarot, came to trial, his friends escorted him from the Black Bull Inn in the Grassmarket bearing a Tree of Liberty "shaped like the letter M" with a scroll inscribed "Liberty, Virtue, Reason, Justice and Truth". And the Tree still exercised its spell in Scotland in the year after Burns's death during the agitation against the 1797 Militia Act, which provided for the conscription of 6000 men between the ages of nineteen and twenty-three: trees of Liberty were set up at Galston and Dalry in Burns's native Ayrshire.[43] There seems no reason, then, why "The Tree of Liberty" should not have been written in 1794 or even 1795, when the emblem was very noticeable in London. In that year a certain "Citizen Lee" had several premises called "The British Tree of Liberty" in Haymarket and Soho, "where may be had variety of cheap Patriotic Publications" with inspiring titles like "King Killing", "The Reign of the English Robespierre", and "The Happy Reign of George the Last".[44] Nevertheless, the Scottish poem does not with any certainty refer to events later than 1793. It is plain from Stanza V that it must have been written after the regicide of 21 January, but the fact that there is no mention of Marie Antoinette does not prove it earlier than her execution on 16 October. Indeed, it is rather improbable that it was composed during the spring of the year, which saw the desertion of Dumouriez and disaster after disaster for the French armies. Stanza VI seems to refer to the victories that followed Robespierre's accession to power at the end of July — Hondschoote on 8 September; Wattignies on 16 October (the very day of the Queen's execution); the suppression of the royalist counter-revolution in Lyons; all French soil liberated from the invader; Belgium reconquered; Holland invaded; and perhaps even the crowing victory of Fleurus on 26 June 1794. Lines 23-4 could conceivably refer to the September massacres in the prisons of 1792, though the poet may also have had the Robespierrian Terror in mind; and line 50 ("Her sons did loudly ca', man") surely points to the first *levée en masse* of the nation in arms, announced on 23 August 1793. The internal evidence, then, points in the direction of late 1793, with the spring of 1794 a possibility.

If "The Tree of Liberty" is not by Burns, it must be either a literary forgery of the 1820s or 30s, or an anonymous composition of the 1790s. If it is a forgery, then we must ask — what known Scots writer of these decades had the necessary talent and the political sympathies to write it? Not Hogg: his detestation of the Revolution was as profound as Scott's, or indeed Boswell's. Not Allan Cunningham, for we have his own statement that he rejected the poem as Burns's on internal evidence. Not Lockhart, for the same reason as Hogg; and surely not Robert Chambers himself, who was thirteen in the year of Waterloo and in his childhood would presumably have imbibed all the anti-French sentiments of wartime Britain, besides − as a serious and dedicated antiquarian − being temperamentally incapable of such an act. If the poem was produced in Chambers's youth, it must have been the work of a talented pasticheur or forger otherwise quite unknown to us.

There are arguments against Burns's authorship which have nothing to do with dating. They are mainly linguistic − the Scots is much "thinner" than one would expect in a poem or song written in this particular measure, and the writer speaks of "England" when at first sight he appears to mean Britain, a fault to which Burns was not prone. Close examination, however, suggests that he is *not* referring to the whole island, but merely to its southern part. It will be remembered that when England is mentioned in the "Ode for General Washington's Birthday", it is in a stanza which begins by apostrophising Alfred, who could never by any stretch of the imagination be described as King of Britain; and when the country is first named, it is deliberately called "thy [i.e. Alfred's] England", to distinguish it from Scotland, which is referred to in the next stanza as "Caledonia". Exactly the same distinction is made in "The Tree of Liberty"; the author really thinks that there are no Trees of Liberty between London and the Tweed, though some have been planted in Scotland (lines 63-4). Immediately before this, the poet writes:

> *Let Britain boast her hardy oak,*
> *Her poplar, and her pine, man!*

And when he says Britain, he means Britain − a unified geographical and political whole with subsidiary parts; he chooses the oak as the traditional symbol of England, and the pine as the emblem of Scotland. The implication of the whole stanza is this: "The Scots agree with the Americans, the French, and many people in Europe − it is only the English who are holding Britain back." The poem can thus be interpreted as − at least in part − a plea to the English to follow Scotland's example.

It will be clear that when "The Tree of Liberty" is considered in the context of Burns's other revolutionary poems, there seems no good reason to reject it on internal grounds, or to dissent from Angellier's judgment:

> It is brutal — bantering and cruel at the same time — like a *sansculotte's* refrain. It is like an echo of *Ça ira*. [Stanza v] might even have been chanted by the mob on the way back from seeing the execution of Louis XVI. . . . This is a genuine revolutionary song. Purely out of sympathy with the people, Burns was rendering much more closely [than any contemporary English poet] the accent of the common people impelled into a frenzy of suspicion, frenzy and impetuosity. Some kind of instinct had given him, quite spontaneously, that tone composed of a mixture of dynamic vulgarity, heroic defiance, and cynical mockery.[45]

As political reaction set in with the trials of such Scottish leaders as Thomas Muir (26 August 1793, 14 years transportation), the Reverend T. Fysshe Palmer (17 September, 7 years banishment), Adam Skirving (6 January 1794, 14 years transportation), despondency overcame many rank and file reformers, though there were also swings towards optimism amid the general gloom.[46] In his letter to Mrs Dunlop of 12 January 1795, immediately after the passage about the perjured blockhead and the unprincipled prostitute, Burns wrote:

> But our friend [Dr Moore, who had "whined" over the executions] is already indebted to People in power, & still looks forward for his Family, so I can apologise for him; for at bottom I am sure he is a staunch friend to liberty.

It is impossible to miss the irony here: Burns, like Moore, was "indebted to People in power" and had to be careful because of

> *These muvin' things ca'd wives and weans*
> *Wad muve the very hearts o' stanes!*
>> ("Searching auld wives' barrels", lines 5-6)

In view of his "apology" for Dr Moore, too, we should take with a very large grain of salt any subsequent criticism of France or the Revolution by Burns in prose or verse. And his next — and last — sentence indicates that he felt freer then than for some time past to say and write what he really felt:

> Thank God, these London trials have given us a little more breath, & I imagine that the time is not far distant when a man may freely blame Billy Pit, without being called an enemy to his Country.

The London trials were those of the bootmaker Thomas Hardy, founder of the London Corresponding Society, who was acquitted of High Treason on 22 November 1794; John Thelwall, of the Society of Friends of the People, acquitted on 5 December; and four lesser figures who were found not guilty on 1 December.

   Thus Burns's emotions fluctuated according to the political climate. We have already noted that the pessimistic "Ode for General Washington's Birthday" was written at various times between January and June 1794 and polished up later; its mood has sometimes been seen as closely linked to that of the song "A Vision", which from circumstantial evidence must be dated no earlier than September 1794:[47]

> As I stood by yon roofless tower,
>   Where the wa'flower scents the dewy air.
> Where the houlet mourns in her ivy bower,   owl
>   And tells the midnight moon her care:

Chorus:
> A lassie all alone was making her moan,
>   Lamenting our lads beyond the sea:
> In the bluidy wars they fa', and our honor's gane and a',
>   And broken-hearted we maun die. —   must

> The winds were laid, the air was still,
>   The stars they shot alang the sky:
> The tod was howling on the hill,   fox
>   And the distant-echoing glens reply. —

> The burn, adown its hazelly path,
>   Was rushing by the ruin'd wa',
>   Hasting to join the sweeping Nith
>   Whase roarings seem'd to rise and fa'. —

> The cauld, blae north was streaming forth   livid
>   Her lights, wi' hissing, eerie din:
> Athort the lift they start and shift,   Across the sky
>   Like Fortune's favors, tint as win. — Lost as soon as won

> *Now, looking over firth and fauld,*
> *Her horn the pale-fac'd Cynthia rear'd,*
> *When, lo, in form of Minstrel auld,*
> *A stern and stalwart ghaist appear'd. —*   ghost

> *And frae his harp sic strains did flow,*   such
> *Might rous'd the slumbering Dead to hear:* as might have
> *But Oh, it was a tale of woe,*
> *As ever met a Briton's ear. —*

> *He sang wi' joy his former day,*
> *He weeping wail'd his latter times:*
> *But what he said it was nae play,*
> *I winna ventur't in my rhymes. —*   will not

The above text, now standard, is what Burns sent to his other musical publisher, James Johnson, for publication in his *Scots Musical Museum*. It does not, however, contain a stanza describing the Minstrel which was published by James Currie in his great Burns edition of 1800. It is most important for our argument, and for the song's political import:

> *Had I a statue been o' stane*
> *His daring look had daunted me:*
> *And on his bonnet grav'd was plain,*
> *The sacred posy — "Libertie".*

Just as in "Scots Wha Hae", the song's vision spans the old independent Scotland and the Scotland now cowed. From the mention of the Nith and the situation of the ruin on the burn (the Cluden) it is clear that the tower was part of the ruins of Lincluden Abbey, whose associations lie deep in Scottish history: it was the burial place of Margaret, Robert III's daughter and wife to Archibald, Earl of Douglas.[48] The landscape is concrete enough, but generalised to the extent that it draws features from different seasons; thus "hazelly" calls forth a vision of spring or summer leaves, "rushing" and "roaring" befit late autumn or winter, and lines 17-20 give a midwinter rendering of the aurora borealis.

The song contrasts, balances and combines past with present, and blends the female lyric tradition of "The Flowers of the Forest" and all women's songs about their men-folk slain in battle, with the male tradition of heroic minstrel figures whose most popular contemporary expression was Macpherson's Ossian. The first four stanzas set poet and "romantic" milieu over against the agonised lament he overhears; it could be that of Scotia or Caledonia, the quintessence of her nation, and one is reminded of "Thee Caledonia, by wild heaths among" of the "Ode on General Washington's Birthday". The "lost honor" of her refrain echoes the betrayal of Freedom, "the coward's secret breath" and the "palsied arm" of the Ode's final stanza. After line 23 the ghostly form of Burns's "Last Minstrel" counterpoints the girl; his harp jostles with her singing; his woeful Lay is not just for a Scottish ear but for a *Briton's,* so that the disguised reference is to the plight of the reformers' cause in England as well as Scotland. Liberty was once the birthright of English and Scots alike, in Alfred's time and the days of Wallace and Bruce; now, in the 1790s, it has been betrayed in both countries.

By January 1795 it was widely believed that a French invasion was imminent, and volunteer corps for local defence were everywhere founded or revived. Burns joined at the beginning of the year and was for some months a member of the organising committee.[49] The song he then wrote for the Royal Dumfries Volunteers, "Does Haughty Gaul invasion threat?" has been seen by some as an act of apostasy. Nevertheless it has lines which must have seemed suspect to some of his more orthodox comrades:

> . . . *For never but by British hands*
> *Maun British wrangs be righted!*
>
> *The kettle o' the Kirk and State,*
> *Perhaps a clout may fail in't:*   patch
> *But deil a foreign tinkler loon*   tinker
> *Shall ever ca' a nail in't!*   drive
>
> . . . *Who will not sing* God save the King
> *Shall hang as high's the steeple:*
> *But while we sing* God save the King,
> *We'll ne'er forget the People!*   (lines 14-5, 29-32)

Auguste Angellier claimed that with "Does haughty Gaul?" Burns became a patriotic Briton overnight, anticipating – but suddenly and impulsively – the evolution which Wordsworth and Coleridge underwent over a period of several years.[50] The truth seems to have been slightly different – that there may have been an element of expediency in his volunteering, and that he always remained a democrat, with upsurges of pro-French feeling right to the end of his life. Burns continued to write political propaganda, but of a local and particular kind, in the form of election ballads for Patrick Heron of Kerroughtrie, who stood as Whig candidate for the Stewartry of Kirkcudbright in February 1795 and in May-June 1796 when he was again a candidate following the dissolution of Parliament. The first of the Heron ballads is typical of Burns's *public* position, and represents a synthesis of the moods of "A Man's a Man" and "Does Haughty Gaul?"

> . . . *For a' that, an' a' that,*
> *Here's Heron yet for a' that!*
> *The independent patriot,*
> *The honest man, and a' that!*

> . . . *For a' that, an' a' that,*
> *Here's Heron yet for a' that!*
> *A Lord may be a lousy loun,*
> *Wi' ribban, star, and a' that.*

> . . . *For a' that, an' a' that,*
> *Here's Heron yet for a' that!*
> *A House of Commons such as he,*
> *They wad be blest that saw that.*

When it comes down to practical politics, the translation of French ideals into British reality means nothing more nor less than the election of a House of Commons composed of "honest men" and "independent patriots".

That Burns could still express staunch support for the ideas of the Revolution some ten months after joining the Volunteers is proved by the Reverend Josiah Walker's account of a meeting with him in November 1795:

> . . . he gave me an account of his latest productions, and repeated some satirical ballads which he had composed, to favour one of the candidates at the last borough election. These I thought inferior to his other pieces, though they had some lines in which vigour compensated for coarseness. He repeated also his fragment of an *Ode to Liberty,* with marked

and peculiar energy, and shewed a disposition which, however, was easily repressed, to throw out political remarks, of
the same nature with those for which he had been repre-
hended.[51]

If the mysterious "Ode to Liberty" is not some poem which has been
forever lost to us, what was it? Either the "Ode on General Washington's Birthday" or − assuming that Walker was not too precise about
the difference between an ode and a long song in a traditional Scottish
metre set to a traditional Scottish tune − "The Tree of Liberty",
although neither of these pieces is a fragment. In either case, the
inference is clear − eight months before his death (21 July 1796),
Burns's opinions were fundamentally unchanged.

7. Conclusion

1789-95 were the last six years of Boswell's life; 1789-96, the last
seven of Burns's. For both they were years of frustration, of goals only
partly attained, and arguably more so for Boswell because of the
shadow of personal grief; his wife had died in the month before the
storming of the Bastille, a blow from which he never recovered. For
Boswell, too, they saw the collapse of his plans to make a career at the
English bar and the dismal end of all his straining and manoeuvring to
become an M.P. If they were coloured by the worries, financial and
other, of providing for and educating a motherless family, they also
saw in May 1791 the publication of the *Life of Johnson,* the greatest
biography in the English language. Though the *Life* brought him
enhanced celebrity, he was only too aware he was journeying downhill;
the news from Europe seemed no blissful Wordsworthian dawn but an
angry sunset reflecting his own autumnal decadence. He tried to keep
depression at bay by dining out and constantly striving to be the life
and soul of the party; as he alternated between heavy drinking and
abstinence, his appearance coarsened and his health deteriorated −
scorbutic eruptions at the end of 1792, "bumps" on the head (?cysts)
in 1793-4, and then his final six-week illness in April and May 1795:
fever, chills, violent headaches, nausea, a swelling in his bladder
which "mortified", and finally death from uraemia, characterised by
one medical authority as "the result of acute and chronic urinary tract
infection, secondary to postgonorrheal urethral stricture".[52]

For Burns, too, these years saw the appearance of his *magnum opus,* so slight in bulk compared to Boswell's: "Tam o' Shanter", one of the finest medium-length narrative poems ever written, as well as the greatest part of his song writing and editing. The main source of *his* frustration was his chronic disdain of the mediocre lairds and citizens of Dumfriesshire, men and women without a tenth of his personality or talent, who alternately feared and scorned the genius in their midst. Perhaps the most vivid glimpse we have of this class-consciousness comes from Syme's account of a tour he made with Burns through Galloway in the late summer of 1793. One wet evening when Burns was in a foul mood because of bad boots, a "sick stomach", and a violent headache, Syme — in an effort to distract him — showed him Lord Galloway's house across the bay at Wigton:

> He expectorated his spleen against the aristocratic elf, and regained a most agreeable temper — I have about half a dozen of capital extempores which I dare not write — But I may *repeat* and you shall hear them some time — I declare they possess as much point and classical *terseness* if I may so express myself, as anything I can imagine. O, he was in an epigrammatic humour indeed — I told him it was rash to crucify Ld. G— in the way he was doing for tho he might not receive any favours at his hands yet he might suffer an injury.
> (John Syme to Alexander Cunningham, 3 August 1793)[53]

For most of his life Burns had much poorer health than Boswell (apart from the latter's repeated attacks of gonorrhoea), and was often ill during his last year and a half. Headaches, frequent stomach disorders, various rheumatic conditions, tonsillitis, melancholic depressions, and the aftermath of heavy drinking, all took their toll: until very recently the consensus of medical opinion has been that he died of rheumatic fever, with possible terminal bacterial endocarditis.[54]

At first sight the Tory Boswell — by 1789 almost completely committed to English life and English ways, and almost always absent from Scotland — and the radical Burns whose song-collecting and editing were inspired by patriotic fervour, not financial gain, had diametrically opposite political lives. Yet both men had a surprising amount in common. Both were Ayrshiremen, both were sentimental Jacobites, both had a romantic attitude to Scotland's past, and to both the Revolution was a potent symbol in the final stage of their development. Of both Boswell and Burns as political thinkers it can be said they were "ordinary" men expressing ideas which gripped multitudes in an age of cataclysmic change. But Burns's ratiocinative intellect was stronger and shrewder than Boswell's: the latter had great architectonic powers (he could plan a biography which is also an epic), but not Burns's abilities in sustained argument. Professor Danziger is perfectly correct when she says that Boswell's response to the Revolution was "vehement and consistent";[55] one reason he never wavered was because the change in his opinions had taken place *before* 1789 when he made a quite remarkable *volte face* on the general question of parliamentary reform in 1785. He put it this way when writing to the Bishop of Killaloe: "I have been fairly converted by observing that Reformers can agree upon no one Plan, and that all of them have an inordinate spirit of resistance to their Superiors coupled with a desire of power over their inferiors."[56] Corsica Boswell, the writer who had inspired freedom-lovers twenty years before, had become a Lost Leader, a defender of slavery, the enemy of any extension of the franchise.

Such obscurantism might be forgiven if it had produced creative work of any quality, but, as we have seen, it did not. Boswell's anti-revolutionary parodies are trash when set beside even the most mediocre of Burns's election ballads; the conflict of ideologies in *Favras* might well have issued in a moving play if Boswell had had the staying power to finish it and − a very big if indeed − he had been able to prune away the tarradiddle of the "God Save the King" extravaganza at the end of Act IV. "No Abolition of Slavery" has merit in places. But its whole concept of "the Universal Empire of Love" fails to unite its disparate halves, while its generally poor versification and technique are enough to explain why it dropped like a stone from the press, unhonoured and unsung. These works, like the vigorous expression of his views in his letters to Temple, are of documentary interest mainly; they make us imaginatively aware of the thoughts, feelings and prejudices of an "ordinary" reactionary of the 1790s.

Burns, it has been the contention of this essay, was almost as consistent in *his* attitude to the Revolution. True, in January 1793 he assured Graham of Fintry that he had given over supporting France; and true, he was active in the Dumfries Volunteers for half a year and more in 1795. But "these muvin' things ca'd wives and weans" are enough to excuse such tactical retreats, and joining the Volunteers did not involve him in any compromise in the matter of parliamentary reform.

To Boswell the Revolution typified the end of ancient excellence and inherited merit. It stood for tragedy and the destruction of true liberty, the liberty of property, whereas for Burns it was a time of awakening, of a promise that what *he* regarded as true liberty — equality of opportunity, the career open to the talents, the triumph of the common man — was possible of attainment. In Burns's case involvement with the Revolution, combined with Scottish patriotism, was the stimulus for five poems of remarkable quality — "Scots Wha Hae", Scotland's unofficial national anthem; "The Tree of Liberty", the most savagely militant of British revolutionary songs; and "A Vision", which, with the closely associated "Ode on General Washington's Birthday", gives moving expression to the feelings of progressives in years of repression and reaction; and "A Man's a Man for a' That", the "Internationale" of those days and of many Scottish generations since.

1. *The Poems of Robert Fergusson*, edited by M. P. McDiarmid, Scottish Text Society, 2 vols. (Edinburgh and London, 1954-56), I, p. 39.

2. *Boswell's Life of Johnson*, edited by G. B. Hill and L. F. Powell, 6 vols. (Oxford, 1934-50), henceforth cited as *Life*, II, p. 220.

3. Quoted in *The Life and Works of Robert Burns*, edited by Robert Chambers, revised by William Wallace. (Edinburgh, 1896), henceforth cited as Chambers-Wallace, II, pp. 372-3.

4. Quoted in *Boswell: the English Experiment 1785-1789*, edited by I. S. Lustig and F. A. Pottle (New York and London, 1986), p. 250.

5. F. A. Pottle, *James Boswell: the Earlier Years 1740-1769* (New York and London, 1966), henceforth cited as *Earlier Years*, p. 453.

6. Diane J. Ducharme, "The Rest of the Boswells", *Scottish Literary Journal*. Supplement 28 (1988), pp. 70-1.

7. Richard B. Sher, *Church and University in the Scottish Enlightenment* (Edinburgh, 1985), p. 70.

8. For the letters to and from Grange, see *The Correspondence of James Boswell and John Johnston of Grange*, edited by R. S. Walker (New York and London, 1966).

9. For Boswell and Lord Marischal, see *Boswell on the Grand Tour: Germany and Switzerland 1764* (London, 1955), pp. 6-7 and *passim*.

10. Quoted in *Earlier Years*, p. 213.

11. *Boswell's Journal of a Tour to the Hebrides*, edited by F. A. Pottle and C. H. Bennett (New York, 1936), p. 163.

12. See H. W. Meikle, *Scotland and the French Revolution* (Glasgow, 1912), henceforth cited as Meikle, pp. 9-13; and Frank Brady, *Boswell's Political Career* (New Haven and London, 1965), henceforth cited as *Political Career*, pp. 5-7.

13. F. A. Pottle, *The Literary Career of James Boswell* (Oxford, 1929), p. 220.

14. *Political Career*, pp. 175-6.

15. Chambers-Wallace, I, pp. 35ff.

16. The original was an English broadside of the seventeenth century.

17. Chambers-Wallace, I, pp. 212-3.

18. *Earlier Years*, p. 300. For more detail see *Boswell for the Defence 1769-1774*, edited by W. K. Wimsatt and F. A. Pottle (London, 1960), especially the account of the trial of John Reid the sheep stealer, pp. 249-68.

19. *Earlier Years*, p. 47 and *passim*.

20. *Earlier Years*, p. 62 and *passim*.

21. F. A. Pottle, *Boswell and the Girl from Botany Bay* (London, 1938).

22. There is a summary of the events surrounding and following the storming of the Bastille in *The Gentleman's Magazine* for July 1789 (vol. 59, p. 658), while the first executions in Paris and the destruction of châteaux are reported in the number for August (p. 750). Newspaper accounts were available earlier than this.

23. *Gentleman's Magazine*, September and October (vol. 59, pp. 852, 942).

24. The plans are in MS. Yale M 84.

25. J. M. Thompson, *The French Revolution* (London, 1943), p. 192, and *Dictionnaire de Biographie Française*.

26. *Gentleman's Magazine*, February 1790 (vol. 60, pp. 174-5).
27. *The Correspondence of James Boswell with David Garrick, Edmund Burke and Edmond Malone*, edited by Peter S. Baker et al. (New York and London, 1986), pp. 159-60.
28. *The Correspondence of Edmund Burke*, edited by T. W. Copeland et al., 10 vols. (Chicago and London, 1958-78), VI, pp. 295-7.
29. Meikle, pp. 91-2.
30. P. A. Brown, *The French Revolution in English History* (2nd. edn., London 1965), pp. 83-4.
31. *From Boswell: the Great Biographer 1789-1795*, edited by Marlies K. Danziger (New York and London, forthcoming).
32. Danziger, "Anarchy", 1.76. (See Acknowledgments).
33. R. T. Fitzhugh, *Robert Burns* (New York, 1970), pp. 377-8.
34. Fitzhugh, pp. 218-20. See also H. W. Meikle, "Burns and the Rosamond", *Burns Chronicle* 1934, pp. 43-52.
35. Fitzhugh, pp. 221-2 (note).
36. Meikle, pp. 103-4.
37. Note from Syme to Alexander Peterkin, cited Fitzhugh, p. 226.
38. From a letter of Syme's, cited Fitzhugh, p. 373.
39. Chambers-Wallace, IV, pp. 132-3.
40. Auguste Angellier, *Robert Burns: La Vie, Les Oeuvres*, 2 vols. (Paris, 1893), II, p. 216.
41. William Roscoe, "O'er the vine-covered hills and gay regions of France", recited on 14 July 1791, the very anniversary which had so perturbed Boswell. It is in Roscoe, *Poetical Works* (Liverpool, 1853), pp. 104ff.
42. *1789:* an exhibition of posters arranged by the Ministry of Foreign Affairs, Paris, 1988, caption to poster no. 18.
43. Meikle, pp. 96, 145, 179-82.
44. For Citizen Lee, see E. P. Thompson, *The Making of the English Working Class* (2nd. edn., London, 1968), p. 158; and for quotations from some of the publications with his imprint, see T. Crawford, "Political and Protest Songs in eighteenth-century Scotland: part 2, 'Songs of the Left'", *Scottish Studies*, vol. 14 (1970), pp. 106-31.
45. Angellier, II, pp. 203-5.
46. For one of these swings see the Government Spy's report in Meikle, p. 136, also pp. 146-8.
47. Burns *Letters*, II, pp. 308-9 and note.
48. *The Poems and Songs of Robert Burns*, edited by James Kinsley, 3 vols. (Oxford, 1968), III, p. 1497.
49. Fitzhugh, p. 358; Burns, *Letters*, II, p. 344.
50. Angellier, II, pp. 206-7.
51. Fitzhugh, p. 360.
52. W. B. Ober, *"Boswell's Clap" and other Essays*, (Carbondale, S. Illinois, 1979), p. 28.
53. Cited in Fitzhugh, p. 367.
54. Fitzhugh, p. 11.
55. "Anarchy", p. 64.
56. Letter of 1 July, 1785 (MS Yale L 42).

ACKNOWLEDGMENTS

I am particularly grateful to Professor Marlies K. Danziger for letting me see the typescript of her article "Horrible Anarchy: James Boswell's View of the French Revolution", in *Studies in Scottish Literature* (vol. 23, 1988, pp. 64-76), cited in the notes as "Anarchy"; and to both the Yale Boswell Office and Professor Danziger for allowing me to read uncorrected proofs of *Boswell: the Great Biographer 1789-1795*, the last volume in the trade series of the Yale Editions of the Private Papers of James Boswell of which she is the editor. I must also thank the publishers and Yale University for letting me quote from Boswell's Journals as published in the McGraw Hill/Heinemann trade edition, and Yale University for all quotations from manuscripts in the Boswell Collection. (The latter are identified parenthetically by their numbers in the Yale Boswell Catalogue). Extracts from Boswell's correspondence as published in *Letters of James Boswell*, edited by C. B. Tinker, 2 vols. (1924) and *The Letters of Robert Burns*, edited by J. de Lancey Ferguson and G. Ross Roy, 2 vols. (1985), are printed by kind permission of Oxford University Press. Quotations from Burns's poetry are from *The Poetry of Robert Burns*, edited by W. E. Henley and T. F. Henderson, 4 vols. (Edinburgh, 1896).